310:
In The Building

A Year in the Life
of a Public School Teacher

Chris Alper

DEDICATION

to Cecile,
always

ACKNOWLEGEMENTS

Thank you to…

the students — for the gift of your attention

teachers and staff of the 310 — for your wisdom

my family and friends — for your unwavering support

CONTENTS

INTRODUCTION

There are very few equivalents to a working life in the classroom: the day-in day-out, unrelenting demand stream, the attention to detail required to survive, the emotional leadership required to carry groups of reluctant and diverse personalities towards a distant goal.

I decided to write this book to tell the story of that world, as I experienced it. It's not a paean to heroic teachers, (except a couple) or a rant designed to tear down the embattled institutions of American public education.

It's just the teaching life, as I lived it. My main hope is that for three groups of people, this book will provide a glimpse into a year In The Building. First, for teachers: so that they can read this and feel like maybe I got it right. Second, for people who know, love and care about teachers: so they can understand at least in some small way, the world teachers leave for every morning. Third, anyone who thinks they could just walk into a classroom and teach.

Sometimes, people decide they can't teach any more: there are many ex-teachers in the world, people who have Been There, facing 60 pairs of eyes evaluating, watching every movement, looking for a window, an advantage, an escape. Full disclosure—I'm one of those ex-teachers.

I spent eight years in the classroom, and it was the most challenging, rewarding and brutal experience I ever had. Triumph, caring, frustration, pain, sadness, simple numbness—all those feelings, sometimes in a single day. I was so tired I considered taking Provigil (a drug originally designed to keep military pilots awake) until the doctor said he had patients who used it, but some were beginning to hear voices not their own.

I was hearing voices not my own anyway. The voices of the kids, as I lay sleepless, thinking. How would the next day be different? How could I change up that algebra lesson? How could I keep them engaged? Could I have said something different to that kid, and kept them in the room for one more hour?

An older teacher once told me, "In your classroom, you make the weather. You are the experience they have." Not a lot of jobs are like that. In the end, we were all in the rooms alone —another unique aspect of teaching, its solitary nature, unexpected in a building stuffed with adults and kids. The principals struggled with this, offering methods for improving the classroom, yet knowing that the minute the bell rang and doors shut, each classroom was like a 19th century warship: each teacher a captain, and a law unto themselves.

By the way, I don't think suburban schools are easier. What I loved about the kids I taught was that you knew where they stood. Often right in front of you, arguing. Suburban kids would be better at hiding things. The parents I met basically trusted me to do my job, and respected teaching, which is most decidedly not the case for many middle- and upper-middle class parents, and certainly a majority of my state's legislators.

I'm not In the Building anymore. I moved in search of a life by the sea, didn't find a teaching job, and went back to the corporate world. I think I would have left eventually anyway, because every year there was a higher caseload, and the only way I felt like I was doing the job any justice was all-in, 150 percent, four nights a week on paperwork and preparation, grading half of every Sunday, about an 85-hour a week. By the time I left teaching, I had plantar fasciitis, a mild skin allergy to dry erase markers, and an unspecified inflammation of several internal organs. Still, I wouldn't trade the experience for anything. I had learned a demanding craft, my world had widened, and the kids had somehow helped me become a better person than I thought I could be.

Other teachers might feel echoes of these stories in their work at a poorer, truly inner-city school; in the wide, well-lit halls of a megalopolis-sized suburban high school; or on the historic campus of an ivy-covered private institution. Kids may see connections with their schools, rural, suburban or Catholic. I hope that's the case, at least, because some parts of all of this are universal. These pages simply describe a school year as I experienced it, 185 instructional days, each of which could feel like an eternity, yet passed in a flash.

When does a teacher's year begin? It actually starts somewhere in the sleepy, hazy depths of late summertime.

SUMMER

Guilt

The first summers were the worst, especially as a career changer with no long history of taking two months off. In my first couple years of teaching, once the infinite relief of summer sank in, I woke up each day with the odd sensation of *not* having to drive frantically off to make it into the hall before the 7:45 bell, *not* worrying about the IEP documents I hadn't written, the giant pile of papers I *didn't* have to prep for my classes.

During the school year, by May I was already fantasizing about my summer break: the great intellectual projects I would undertake, (this summer I think I'll reread Shakespeare, or study the War of 1812, or write a book, or learn Sanskrit), mentally listing the dozens of house projects (gutters, refinish the porch, hang doors, paint the entire house, lift it off its foundations with my bare hands, the usual) or vowing to get in shape (I'll run a marathon—usually by August downgraded to running down to the park.) Into this mental frenzy I interlaced the requirements of my kids' lives in the summer (take my son to day camp, take my daughter everywhere within a 400-square mile area at least once to play music).

My wife told me to relax, but I felt guilty because she was at work and I wasn't. "How are you?" she'd ask, during a lunchtime call, and I'd rattle off a spastic litany of tasks I had completed, planned out, or was about to begin, along with minor injuries sustained in the process. There'd be a brief silence, and then she, ever wise, would say, "You need to chill."

My sister- and mother-in-law, as veteran teachers, became my role models and sanity checks. I'd be covered with sawdust, an unopened history of the Spanish-American War on the kitchen table, stuffing two crackers with cheese in my mouth to serve as lunch, a partly-hung door blocking the hallway. I'd have one eye on the clock, because it was almost time to get my son from half-day theater camp, when I'd get a call from my sister-in-law, looking for my wife, maybe planning one of our vacations out west.

"So, what's up?" I'd ask her. "Oh not much," she'd say, an icon of calm after 20 summers off. "I was reading the New Yorker. Maybe later I'll bake some cookies." My mother-in-law, a retired veteran of 35 years teaching high school French, might also call, looking for my wife. I'd tell her what I was doing, and she'd say, "Relax, sweetie, you've earned a rest."

But after working continuously since the age of 12, when I started pulling weeds at a ranch down the street, I had huge trouble with that concept. Ranch hand, paper boy, sailboat delivery crew, busboy, dishwasher, ice cream parlor counter guy, lifeguard, library assistant, writer, editor, archaeology assistant, copywriter, boatyard worker, help desk technician, middle manager, teaching aide, tutor, coach, schoolteacher— of those, teacher was the only job on my life list that came with a 10-week vacation.

It messed with my mind. I knew I needed the time off. By June 15th every year, wonderful as my work was, and however much I cared about my students, I felt like my soul had been beaten with a rubber hose in a small room under the dim light of a single bulb.

I'd go out in public after 9 a.m. every day, and once in line at the coffee shop, remembering that I hadn't shaved in a couple of days, wonder if the baristas thought I was unemployed. I started wearing a t-shirt I bought when I was getting my license, with the name of my university and School of Education written proudly across it. (See, I'm not between jobs, I'm a teacher!) Sometimes I'd carry the teacher's edition of my algebra or science textbook with me, displaying it spine-side out on my coffee shop table as I read something else entirely. Usually it wasn't Shakespeare or the history of medieval ship design, it was a beat-up used copy of a military science fiction series or a windsurfing magazine.

I'd go to pick my son or daughter up at whatever camp or activity they were attending, and there were two different Looks I'd get. The Mid-Day Look: at the back door of the

Children's Museum, or Chamber Music Camp, or the Children's Theater; came from either Organized Mom, roughly the same age as me (perfect hair, yoga clothes and mat, clean SUV), Harried Mom, (many young children, dirty mini-van) or Summer Nanny (college girl, hair in ponytail, earbuds in).

It was a quick assessment: was this middle-aged, off-white Male—6'2", unshaven, dressed like a 25-year-old surfer in shorts and Hawaiian shirt, driving a small, dirty Toyota with roof racks—a creepy predator? Probably not, he's carrying a copy of Hamlet. Though he hasn't read it, apparently, the receipt is still tucked inside the front cover like he just bought it.

The Afternoon Look came from Dad, in pressed, collared shirt, summer-weight slacks, dress shoes with tassels, who also appraised me. It was the same thing basically, except with the added judgement that though I wasn't a child molester, because I wasn't leaning on a white conversion van, I was definitely an unemployed left-wing intellectual. It was the Hamlet, which he had been forced to read at the U, and which irritated him because the language didn't make any sense. Dad managed this as he stayed on a conference call, hugged his children, and handed them into a Lexus. Fine multi-tasking.

By the sixth summer, though, I was at peace with it all. I had a shorter list of house projects, was done with Hamlet, and had moved on to the Tempest. I learned to cook, and when I got a Look at the back door of the Children's Theater I took my sunglasses off to look back, and smile.

Teachers survive, 185 days at a time, one school year at a time, and blessed be, one summer at a time as well. I was never entirely guilt-free, but as a recovering Catholic, I don't think I'd be entirely comfortable with that. In the meantime, I ignored the back porch refinishing another day, read a little, defrosted a chicken to cook later, and, whoa, look at the time, it was time to pick up the lad from Children's Theater.

Work Week

Long days, free and clear, spent in the company of your own children, instead of other people's. An ocean of time, exploring things that matter to you. A teacher's summer.

I started June like a runner shuffling through the last two miles of a marathon, physically and mentally spent. By late July, I was recovered, human again, my mind no longer racing at three a.m., my body no longer filled with more caffeine than a church basement during a pancake breakfast.

But around that time, the clouds started to form. A nameless small dread. The clenching of an inner fist, commingled with the return of the unquenchable passion. I'd start to think. (This year I could...Maybe if I try this vocab method...) I'd pick up a book or two, and start to believe again. By early August school was on my mind. When I thought of how much time was left, I thought in days, then hours. I wrapped up the last small projects in the garage and the garden, finished the last book.

Somehow, without any real time having seemed to pass, it was the weekend before Work Week, teacherese for the days we worked before classes commence. In my school email, which I opened for the first time since June, is the schedule of activities. What I will do the first day, the first week, the time before the buses roll up and the kids get off, some in their brand new uniforms, others with the cool eyes of veterans, shirts and shorts worn by a year or two of washing, appraising, measuring. But for now, the kids are not yet there.

The weekend passed. I barbecued, got to a day game one more time at Target Field, looked around my house to find the lanyard I had laid away with reverence and joy in June, its click and sway not to be felt all the long, lazy summer. Sometimes, even when I was with my family, my mind started to go down the path, the well-worn track that helped me survive the year. They saw my eyes were distant, thinking— what's the best way to get that third-period math class to do better this year...I hope there's enough room in the new room for my tables. My family knew soon I would be gone again.

Monday came. I geared up and got in the car, hung the lanyard in its place, drove slowly, down roads not yet filled with school morning traffic, over roads that curved and twisted and led me inexorably to the school. It's the same route I'd drive, through snow and ice and rain, all through the year, and at the same time down to the minute, to get me to The Building.

I pulled up in the lot. People getting out. Rolling suitcases. Backpacks. Nods and smiles and handshakes. I held my ID up to the door lock, in the back, out by the gym stairs entrance. The hallways were quiet and clean. No clouds of Axe cologne, torn-up papers or slamming lockers. Not yet.

They were out there, somewhere. Of course, since they

were middle-schoolers, they were not at all thinking they'd be here in a week. They were thinking of the Now, a trait I admire and strive towards, but no amount of Zen mediation can slow down the passage of time the way it can for a 13-year-old mind, not yet worn down by the harness traces of responsibility and adult life.

I opened the door of my room. Boxes were piled everywhere, tables stacked in the corner: staff must have cleaned the carpets. The room smelled a little musty, dry and cool. Sounds echoed in the corners. I slid open the battered grey metal of the desk, the top drawer, the one full of things I'd found. Shiny glittery pencils with unicorns for erasers. CDs of pop singers with Hispanic names. A comic book. Drawings of manga characters left on the floor, (common) or given with a dedication "to Mr. A." (rare).

I closed the drawer, locked the door and headed up to the library. Saw everyone now—Hey, how's it going? How was your summer? What did you do? Take any cool trips? How are your kids? Me, nope kept it quiet this summer, actually went out east. That a new car? Yeah? How you like that?

Took a seat in the library. Coffee, donuts, fruit. Administrators jacked up. For them, this is Game Day. Work week is the one and only time in the year they get full attention. It's their chance to impart methods, strategies and messages they've been developing frantically all summer. The coaches and curriculum people from the school district, almost foaming at the mouth with their eagerness to get the New Thing into the hands of the people who can Change Outcomes for Kids, drifted uneasily in the back of the library.

The New Thing Which Will Change Outcomes for Kids is going into place this day, and our test scores will rise, hallelujah, praise be the New Thing.

The principal conferred at the front of the room with the Building Coach. She was ready to roll—a good principal, her heart in the right place, and she cared about the kids. But she was only a principal, after all. My hands, and the hands of the people around me, were the ones that built the Ark we all sailed upon.

A few New People sat scattered throughout the crowd. Some have been welcomed by their departments. Some were Come Backs, returned to our school from a posting elsewhere—another middle school, maybe high school or elementary, now back in the middle. Some were First-Years. Scrubbed clean, radiating idealism. Thank God for them. Their eyes would focus a little more tightly next Tuesday, when their souls went into the crucible to face the blast-furnace pressure that was the reality of the classroom. But not today. Today they wondered if they could really do this, if they were up to the whole thing. A few didn't worry, and were filled with confidence. Those were the ones who broke.

The principal stepped up, turned on the mic and started the school year. "Welcome back everyone! I hope you had an awesome summer, I did. I'm fired up, glad to be back, and this year we are headed for a new place, together..."

The second day I often had district meetings. Once, when we had a new superintendent, every teacher in the district congregated. It was pretty cool—we filled a sports arena in downtown Saint Paul, all 4,500 of us. Then I had meetings

9

for all special education teachers, which during my early years was a couple hundred, but year after year of budget cuts resulted in that group later being barely enough people to fill a high school cafeteria.

By the third day, I was becoming anxious to get into my room, prep some packets, make my posters, lay out the tables, get ready. People needed to get into their rooms the same way a chef needs to sharpen knives, mince scallions, and fire up the burners. They were coming. The kids were coming.

People started to skip meetings, stay late, especially the people who moved (in any given year, the majority of people in my school moved classrooms).

If I was lucky, I got a few hours in my room, and ended up ready as I could be. Unpack, sort out, reload. The air was humid, despite the A/C. The room was quiet, like it wouldn't be again for nine months. No drama had yet played out here. I looked around the room and thought about the months to come—flipped the switch, locked the door and headed up the stairs to the parking lot. Labor Day weekend. One last barbecue. Work Week was done.

When I came back Tuesday, it was on.

FALL SEMESTER

SEPTEMBER

The Honeymoon

The room was perfect, ready to roll, everything in its place. The first bell rang and I was standing at the door. The kids filed down the hallway, and I watched them coming around the corner. Many held schedules before them, crisp and new, like talismans warding them against this unfamiliar world. By Day Four, after dozens of consultations, they will be worn-out, soft-edged paper rags.

The kids peered at the schedules, then the door plates, trying to divine the relationship between our room numbering system, apparently developed by an insane numerologist with an opium habit, and the place they are supposed to be. In seven years, I never figured out the connection between the numbers and the rooms. Once, I was in Room 7101, and the room across the hall was 37B. The room next door to that was 2300. I had a paper taped up on the wall, telling kids my name and what classes are in the room during which period.

I welcomed them, shook their hands, pointed out their assigned seats. They dropped into the desks in dozens of different ways–fast and graceful, slow and awkward, hesitant, surly, bouncy, shy–but, gradually, they settled in. A couple faces turned toward me with natural, smiling openness; most regarded me and the other kids with careful neutrality, assessing; one looked away, his street face on, his "don't mess with me" look in place. The bodies were twitchy, jumpy, especially the seventh-graders. They'd been hearing stories from neighborhood kids, old schoolmates; telling them, "It isn't like elementary up in there. It's complicated. You got to move around a lot." There were bigger kids in this building, like their tough older cousins. They were thinking about all of this.

For some kids, the school was ridiculously safer and more tranquil than the homes they lived in. For a handful of kids, white-collar outliers who arrived after last-minute parental business relocations, then typically transferred out to nearby private schools, my school seemed like another world. For kids recently arrived in the US, the school was a drift dive through a babble of foreign words; all English, all the time. The teachers they understood sometimes, their own people all the time, most of the other kids not at all. Somali girls looked out at me from under their school-issue blue headscarves, drab and uniformly blue, nothing like the clouds of rainbow they would wear on happier occasions later in the year.

I checked them all against my list. The bell rang, and I stood up in front of the classroom. A couple of kids still talked, but most didn't. I taught them the first thing they would learn from me, the way we would begin countless dialogues over the next nine months.

"My name is Mr. Alper-Leroux. Lotta kids call me Mr. A., since it's easier, but that's up to you." Over the years, after being called Mr. Alpalux and Mr. Alperoo, I added that bit. "There's a little x up here on the floor, which I made out of masking tape. You'll also see I have a picture of a traffic light up behind me." The teaching light was a PowerPoint I made—three slides, graphics showing red, yellow and green traffic lights—projected one at a time up on the screen in front of my room. "When it's red, I'm talking, and no one else is speaking except me and whoever I might be talking to." I switched the slide. "When it's yellow, you are talking only to each other, in small groups at your table. You aren't talking to people in any other part of the room." I switched the slide again. "When it's green, you are speaking to each other politely, in normal inside voices." I switched it back to red.

"So here's your cue when we are going to get to work. I ring this bell," and I slapped a hotel call bell I had up on my front table, "and I say, 'I'm up on the x, and the light is red', and we start." One kid immediately asked, "What happens if we talk?" I answered, "If it's just you, I write your initials up on the whiteboard, and you get 30 seconds at the end of class. You wait here after the bell rings, then go on to your next class. If there are so many people talking I can't figure out who it is, everyone gets 30 seconds. Usually, I give you a chance to earn the 30 seconds back by how you handle yourselves the rest of the day. Everyone understand? If you get this, please say yes so I can hear you." I made sure I heard everyone say yes. One kid didn't. I waited. "Everyone." He said yes after a few seconds. They were checking to see if I meant what I said.

"Ok, so…" **ding**, I rang the bell, "I'm up on the x and the light is red, and I'm going to…"

"Mr A.?"

"One more thing—in here you raise your hand if you'd like to ask a question. I might not call you right away, but I'll remember that you want to talk to me. This time, T., that's a free pass, next time it'll be 30 seconds. Don't worry, you'll get this figured out. Right now we are going to look at the weekly calendar…"

T. turned to his tablemate, and said quietly, "That 30 seconds is bogus." I glanced briefly at the seating chart, quickly wrote up the kid's initials, TJ. "T., that's 30 seconds. You can earn it back. Now we're going to go over how this class works."

T. raised his hand. I continued, "I'm going to tell you how you'll know what to do each day in this class." The hand was still up, and his foot started to tap impatiently. "Turn to the second page, please." I moved from the front of the class to stand by T., as the kids turned the pages,. "What's up, T.?"

"How you gonna hold me here for 30 seconds?", he said. I told him, "Just how it is. We have lots of work to do, you guys have a lot to learn this year, keeps everything moving."

A few of the other kids pretended to be looking at the papers, others watched us openly. They were listening, judging. "T., we're on page 2." I waited, watched him slowly turn to page 2. I returned to the front of the class.

I reset expectations. "So I'm up front, the light is red, no one talks except me and the person I might be talking to." I waited. The room was quiet. "Page 2 shows you the week's schedule. What we'll do in class, then what the homework is." As I talked, I scanned the room. T. was following along, but I knew the signs. Anyone willing to go up against the system on Day 1 would likely be crashing against all the limits I set by the end of the week.

No problem. I trusted my system, and though many kids would spend an extra 30 seconds (or minute, or 90 seconds) waiting after the bell over the course of the year, it all worked out pretty well. They had four minutes of passing time, and the school wasn't large, so they'd get where they needed to be by the next bell. It just cut into their socializing time, which is why it was so effective.

Minute by minute, the first blocks in the foundation of our year together were laid. There were literally dozens more that established the flow, the ground rules, the climate in the classroom. That's what the honeymoon time was for. The testing went on, hour after hour, over the course of the first days. They were watching for cracks, chinks in the armor, leaks in the little rowboat of learning we would share for the next 185 days.

For the kids, establishing the system was the most boring part of the year; for me, it was the most critical, even for something like going to the bathroom. I told them they couldn't go in the first 10 minutes or last 10 minutes of class, and they could go once a week. I kept a list.

Kids with any excuse to go to the nurse would try that out at least once in the first week—diabetes, meds, asthma, allergies, "my stomach hurts."

I would see a handful of these kids more than half of each day; some for two periods of reading, a period of math, and a period of science. I spent more time with those particular kids during the mid-day hours than their parents. For that reason alone, they watched me especially carefully.

The first couple of years I taught, when the first few days went smoothly, I went home and told Cecile, "Maybe this year will be quiet. They seem like a good group." After a few years in the classroom, though, I knew that what happens during the first week's honeymoon is no indication at all what the arranged relationship between you and the dozens of kids you see every school day would be like.

The small rebellions that would soon flower out into the open, blaze out into the hall, burst into the office crying, still simmered quietly. The reality was this: in the first few days, they had not yet begun to fight.

Being Mr. A.

Whoever Mr. A. was, he wasn't me. At least, not all of me. He spoke with greater volume, in clipped sentences, and said things like "You got to...", "Here's the thing...", and "Focus up front." He connected with the kids, somehow, using all his experiences: some from growing up in an odd kind of highly-educated lower-middle class rural neighborhood on a tropical island, amongst drunks and drug addicts, PTSD-ed vets and Utopia seekers, hippies and Hawaiians. He guided the kids in a carefully-plotted, research-based arc towards where they had to go. He was organized, meticulous.

Mostly, he had no personality at all, at least for a while. He was The System in his room, determined to get the work done. He was all about that.

He was a better person than me, since he couldn't get mad, couldn't be impatient and always had to try to get the best out of people. He never gave up on a kid—ever, no matter what. He worked incredibly hard to be fair.

Of course, the reason he was all these things is because if he wasn't, the super-pressurized world of his classroom would explode in a heartbeat. There is nothing more unstable, not the highest atomic number there is–Californium, Francium, whatever–than a middle-school classroom without a smooth system. He felt like the concrete lid on the reactor at Three

Mile Island—purposeful, pushed, and cracking.

He had experience in the classroom enabling him to instantly find solutions, share scarce resources, discover ways to handle conflict, reassure, push, cajole and hold the line. He cared about the kids, more than he let on. He thought maybe somehow they knew.

He was always surprised when a kid felt strongly positive about him. He didn't feel like he did anything special for anyone. He tried never to talk down to a kid. He never felt that much different than them—they were him at 12 and 13, a little lost, growing up mostly unsupervised—a bit wild.

There were things he could say that were true, and points of connection. He'd had a single mom; he knew people who had lived lives including minor crime. Sometimes he'd leave ambiguity. Like one time when the kids talked about handcuffs and he said, "The thing I hate is when you are in the squad car, the handcuffs make it hard to sit back." They laughed, thinking he was joking. Then maybe wondering a little. He loved sports, and had in full measure the inner 13-year-old carried around by every adult male that enjoyed action movies and video games.

He talked about these things sometimes, not in large group where they were a welcome distraction, but in small group when few could hear. He tried to make the class interesting, every day. He knew if he was bored, they'd be bored. He tried to bring his best every minute.

In his teacher training, he had been told that extrinsic rewards did not work. But in his first year, he found the opposite, when he met a veteran teacher who ran a store.

Kids earned points for doing necessary things in class, then once a week they could buy small candies, chips, pencils or other items with their points. He immediately made a store. Store taught the kids all kinds of lessons, and Mr. A. was able to teach kids money-related lessons using the store, which made him happy. His kids were going to need a lot more than basic math and reading to get by in their world. Store was an economic system as tightly regulated as a Swiss bank, because the kids watched every transaction.

How he was perceived by the kids, he still has no idea. He is pretty sure he was not adored, as some were, but neither was he despised. The highest praise he ever got was something he heard in a hallway, coming from around a corner, one kid talking to another kid. Mr. A. was not visible.

The first kid said, "Who you got for Earth Science?"

The other replied, "Mr. M., he's the bomb."

"Yeah."

"Wait, isn't that the class with the two teachers? That for real?"

"Yeah, the other one's Mr. A. He's alright."

I could do worse for praise.

Sleeplessness and strategy

Before November, I never slept through the night. I would awaken in the early morning, the house quiet, radiators ticking softly, maybe some wind in the leaves of the trees outside our bedroom window: thinking, plotting, recalibrating, moving furniture in my mind—lost in an internal monologue.

"I need to move J., she's too close to X. Maybe if I moved the tables from right by the front of the room, they wouldn't clash on the way out, even if I dismissed by rows." I thought about how I could put a table with two chairs in the back, out of the line of sight for S., who liked to stare at other kids while my back was turned until they got irritated. Then I had to handle the kid who had become irritated, without seeing the source of the trouble. Eventually, I figured it out it was S. who was causing the trouble.

I knew I had to shift everything, to stay moving, one step ahead, float like a butterfly, but don't sting like a bee, keeping the more creatively troublesome kids off balance. It was the one advantage I had—I could change the world. They'd roll in, looking for a gap, a missing piece, an inconsistency. I never blamed them or took it personally. If learning challenges made my school days incredibly difficult (at best) and brutal (at worst), I'd do that too. Also, they were just kids, and that's what kids do in school. All teachers had slack in their system somewhere, and the kids were on a mission to find it.

I was never sure if any of the other teachers stayed awake, replaying what had happened, thinking about what they could have done better, said differently, about how they could improve a lesson. They might have, but I never asked, and it wasn't really something you could share. Teacher Code includes a pretty clear unspoken mandate to handle yourself as though everything is going fine, that You Got This, that it's all under control. You might share a couple of thoughts with your friends, but to most people, you are all good, maintaining an even strain.

It occurred to me, about three years in, I was actually only thinking about the situations I had mishandled or the ones that had gone haywire. That meant there were literally dozens I'd handled right, because there really were that many interactions in a single day. Sometimes I remembered a word choice, an alternative I had offered, material I had altered for a kid, a conversation with another adult that had kept a kid on the rails. So at times I did okay. Outside, the wind blew, the rain fell, or the snow drifted, and I contemplated, my family asleep in the house, the school far away.

I'm not an insomniac by nature, but I really did have to figure things out that night, because the next day, they'd all be waiting for me. I had to find the individual points in the line that I would hold: consistent overall, yet different for each kid, for each moment, for each subject. For me professionally, it was the ultimate moving target, especially compared with performance standards at other jobs I had held. The consequences of a lack of skill or inspiration was an unstable situation, which could result in a kid losing a concept, a period, or even a day of school. If I handled a scenario well, they worked harder, learned more, and stayed in class. If not, it was another idea, moment, or day lost on their educational journey.

Over the years I taught, I had roughly 200 students I was individually responsible for. If you throw in my co-teaching, probably around 500 total. In that time there was only one kid who completely circumvented everything I could think of to get him to be a part of the class, stay in the flow and learn what he needed to learn.

We can call him D. I first worked with him in the spring of 2011. My principal asked if I could take over a math class that had already gone through two teachers that year, and the kids had gone completely feral. The very first day I ran the class, a girl got up and threw a desk across the room.

D. made his entrance the next day. He came in, all attitude and swagger, and sat where I had placed him, second row, second from the front, on the right. This was my Eyes On position. If you put a kid all the way in the front, they felt singled out. All the way on the left and it was too easy for them to escape out into the space. That year my "room" was a curtained-off space that was part of a huge area that used to be the wood shop, before budget cuts took the machines away. He sat down, I gave him the math packet ("every lesson by day, minimum number of problems highlighted, if you lose it, I've got plenty of others.") He looked at it, flipped a page, closed it ostentatiously.

I let it ride. He was establishing his cred, through his indifference, publicly. I decided I'd loop back with him after I finished introducing the concept. We did the warm-up, and I was watching the room. D. was antsy, sliding down, then back up in his seat. His head swiveled around, eyes scanning the other kids. Far left row, three seats back, on the outside, was SH, a goofy kid with a huge natural Afro that was his pride and joy. He was impulsive, said ridiculous things sometimes, but was basically a good kid. I was a couple of minutes into my explanation of order of operations when D. took off out of his seat after SH, desks flying as he leapt across the room.

Somehow, I was just there, and managed to get an arm over D.'s shoulder enough to turn him, (using some anger management training I'd picked up in professional development as an aide) and the punch he threw at SH missed. SH was stunned, because even by the Kid Code, whatever he had whispered under his breath to D. wasn't anywhere near a fighting offense. Even as a seventh grader, though compact, D. was very strong. I walked D., my arm still over his chest, towards the door, calling out over my shoulder for the aide to get on the phone and call the AP.

That was the beginning of a 15-month relationship. I was his case manager, and he did have a learning disability, but mostly he was a ball of rage and restlessness. Over the next year and a half, I tried an incredible number of things. I changed his schedule five or six times. I had parallel work for him. I arranged to have a blow-up signal for him in other classes. He ended up in as many of my own classes as I could get him—math, reading, science, so I could keep an eye on him four out of six periods. I moved his desk, had alternate assignments, had him on teams with friends, strangers, alone.

He was suspended three times for fighting and confrontations with staff by the end of the first year. By November of the next year, he was suspended twice. He was rarely in class. Once he was just gone for a couple of months, in a nearby small city, with family. He was constantly with Miss M., the social worker, who was pretty close to a saint in how she worked with him (and every other kid who came through her door.)

The one thing he didn't ever do was the work. We tried video lessons, lessons he could draw, spoken-word response; assisted writing using a laptop with sentence prediction software; incentives, strict consequences. Nothing. I knew from his diagnostic tests it would be difficult, but possible, for him to read and do math. Much easier in fact than it was for a lot of my other kids.

We had long talks with Mom, Grandma, the AP, the principal, social workers, district specialists for new strategies, and even people from the county. It wasn't like we were establishing some kind of bond, D. and myself, but neither was it adversarial. I don't think he liked me necessarily, or disliked me, but I'm not sure how much he liked anyone. I think he may have appreciated what I was trying to do, on some level.

It was more like a chess match, teacher vs. student. I always got the first move, but he definitely countered well. His education just wasn't happening, and that was how it was going to stay, from his point of view.

But I can be stubborn sometimes, so every strategy I had ever tried, every method I had used with other kids, I tried on him, and I still lost many, many hours of sleep deciding how to work with D. He was immune. By the end of spring semester in his 8th grade, more than a year after I met him, I knew that in my time with him, there was not going to be some kind of miracle.

Despite my midnight contemplation and arsenal of tricks, the moves and accommodations, parent calls and grandma calls, schedule changes, video lessons and talks at lunch, D. remains in my mind the One Who Got Away.

Sometimes, I wonder where he is now.

Staff

When you count people who work at a school, the teachers are most numerous, but by no means the most important. There are many other people in crucial roles who make a school run smoothly, most of whom don't show up in newspaper stories about education, or in journal articles, but who are critical to the quality of a building's daily life.

Aides

Some of them could have been magnificent teachers. Having been an aide myself, I understood how difficult their role was. For very little money, they worked with us closely, acting as the glue that held our system together. They walked with kids not in control of themselves, counted incidents for records that later became part of teacher-parent conferences, and were a source of comfort for a lot of kids who just can't bring themselves to connect with a teacher. They were not so much older than the kids, like a beautiful young woman named Miss G. who had all the boys entranced, and who used her charm to get them to do their homework; they were life-experienced, like Miss P. a Newfoundlander who needed a cane to walk through the halls, but whose energy when it came to the kids was boundless, and who gave her all every day for them. They were brother/uncle figures, like Mr. M., a street-wise and savvy ex-high school quarterback, who led the kids with smooth style, infinite patience and tremendous heart. They were the closers, the people who smoothed the edges, keeping classes running by handling extremes of emotions so teachers could roll on, maintaining the flow.

Secretaries

Anyone who believes they don't actually run a school has not worked in one. From the first minute of the day to the last, they coordinate, plan, move people, provide institutional memory, counsel kids, connect with kids, manage parents of every disposition, carry forward the tiniest detail for every teacher. They are finders (of people, things, resources and money), keepers (of secrets, keys and paperwork) and they are occasionally weepers, when they connect with a kid who is having trouble getting through the system.

They make events, big and small, run smoothly as a Swiss watch. They are the wind in everyone's sails, and anyone who disrespects them is both a fool and foolish.

Once, as part of a workflow exercise, our principal's secretary sat in the principal's office, and the principal herself got out and roamed the halls. It was, in all the years I worked there, the only time I saw the true practical structure in the school as it was truly constituted. I was, and remain, infinitely thankful for the work they did. I know for a fact I could not have taught without them.

Engineers and Custodians

When their work was poor, as I saw in other schools, the effect on the school was remarkable. It was part and parcel of disenchantment, disaffection and disconnections.

Our school was blessed with an A-List team. The walls and floors were spotless. They somehow managed to clean up the incredible mess left by 800 kids day after day after day. The heat was on, the toilets worked and the lights were steady.

In the world of middle school, where every tiny distraction kept kids from learning, they removed those distractions. They added pride to our environment, and I was always very thankful for them.

I knew a teacher once who attempted to lord it over them. She had a Ph.D. and for some reason felt this made her superior to the custodians. In fact, when they stopped doing all the things they didn't have to do for her to make her life better—when they went letter of the law—the rest of us could see the effects on her room and her teaching.

The custodians and engineers knew everything. People thought because they cleaned rooms they didn't have a clue what was going on, but I suspect they knew as much as the principals and the AP about most of the stories, drama and hidden secrets of the school—archaeologists and social workers wrapped into one. I'm not sure how many people ever asked them, though.

Sometimes towards the end of the year they were irritable, but I could understand that. I would be too if every day I watched the kids lay down a fresh coat of debris, which I had to pick up, week after week, year after year.

Cafeteria

They were called lunch ladies, but they also made breakfast, bag lunches for field trips, snacks for conferences and provided emergency food for kids in need. Most of the time I was at my school, they fed between 600 and 900 kids.

What impressed me was that they did it in the face of a near-universal lack of appreciation, but they still cared. They knew the kids complained, could hear them complain, could see their written complaints on the tables (This food sucks! I wish we had McDonalds!), yet somehow they still stepped up to the serving line. I think they knew a lot of kids were fronting, were saying these things because they were supposed to.

We all knew that for more than a handful of kids, this was the only hot meal they'd get, unless they were in a shelter. For some, it was one of very few meals that didn't come from a convenience store. Of course, most kids were eating with their families, but for many more than I personally would have believed possible, the cafeteria at my school was like a three-star restaurant.

I think the lunch ladies knew who those kids were.

Security

We always had an armed security guard working at the front door. In theory, this person (we had both men and women over the years) was there to guard the entrance, but I remember overhearing one guard saying to the principal and

AP after an intruder drill that if there ever actually was an intruder, he'd be running out the back door. They kind of looked at him like—seriously, we thought that was your job, dude.

He said, "No way I'm dying here in this school for 13 bucks an hour." At least he was honest. Shortly after that, and I'm sure it was just coincidence, we got a new security guard, just as heavily armed, but more approachable. She was good with the kids—firm, but they felt they could talk to her. She became another resource to talk to the kids who couldn't stay in class—Kids in the Hall, as I thought of them. Those were the kids for whom we had to make a patchwork curriculum, woven into time with the social worker, in the behavior room, in the office, while waiting for the principal to talk to them.

I bet she wouldn't have run.

Behavior Specialists

I saw a few over the years, and I thought of them as spiritual lifeguards. The reality was that these folks and the kids they worked with were basically exclusively African-American. There was a lot of focus on that fact, that too many kids of color were being kicked out of class, suspended, and missing their education as a result. I can't claim to know the exact set of causes that led to this. Certainly the school system was a mismatch with some aspects of their culture, and for some of the kids, their family and home lives were so chaotic that they carried their chaos with them. Yet other African-American kids seemed to manage the code switch and function fine.

Whatever the case, the Behavior Specialists settled into a role between Tough Loving Uncle (for the boys) and Tough Loving Older Female Relative (for the girls.)

They took on the Sisyphean challenge of trying to keep a handful of kids in class and on track. They fought with early morning behavior classes for the kids (that was Mr. B.), with after-school basketball teams (Mr. C.), with in-school girl's hour (Miss R.). They never, ever gave up on the kids. They showed up at our doorways and took on the minute-by-minute, mostly thankless task of working just a little more knowledge into a kid who wanted nothing of it.

I'm pretty sure they saved some lives, but I was just a white teacher watching from afar. They were—and are now somewhere—warriors, fighting for the kids against the system and the dominant culture itself. My respect for them is boundless.

Nurses

If My Stomach Hurts was a disease, they would all have been internationally-renowned experts. They medicated, commiserated and listened, and sometimes were our only line of communication into a family.

There were several who served at my school over the time I was there, and though they were very different people, they consistently had the ability to stay unbelievably calm and patient with their hormonally-overdriven visitors.

Like all of the staff, without them we wouldn't have had a true community.

Smells and sounds

I 've read smell is the most powerful of memory prompters: that when a smell from a particular time in your life is re-experienced, you are transported back in time to when it happened, reminded in full force of who and what you were at that time.

For me, the remembered smell of my teaching years has several components. In fact, if you were making a perfume called Eau de Middle School, the scent notes you could not forget would include:

Axe: The go-to scent of boys 14 and under. Usually applied in small oceans just prior to a dance or other social event, with the baseline philosophy that if a little smells good, a lot smells great. I've had my eyes water walking past an open locker, and prior to the Valentine's Day dance, a hazmat suit might not have been a bad idea.

Pizza: As I will discuss later, pizza is the manna of middle school classroom foods. It can be served at least twice a week in a cafeteria, once as lunch, once as breakfast pizza, which I sometimes saw lying around just prior to first period and of which I could not begin to guess the ingredients (eggs?). It's brought as a reward, the main food during Christmas parties, and is a staple of after-school club teachers to keep pre-adolescent blood sugar up in the late afternoon. Its main virtues: simplicity and divisibility. No matter how many kids are in a classroom at any given moment, you are basically presented with a Whole, as I used to describe when teaching math. Splitting that into 16ths, 32nds or even fifths is not a big deal. Also, no utensils required, paper towels for plates. Easy. Smells great, too.

Sweat: Although experienced in the first few days of school (no A/C), after recess, and occasionally for kids with whom you have the OK, So You Know How It Didn't Used to Matter So Much That You Showered Every Day, Well, That's No Longer True conversation, the real pinnacle of sweat smell in middle school was dances. Released from the draconian strictures we placed on them, and thrust into near proximity with the dreaded-feared-adored Opposite Sex, the kinesthetic result was that kids essentially ran in circles for 90 minutes in a closed gym. With 800 other kids. Add in the activities going on in the upstairs gym, connected to the lower gym by stairs, upon which they also ran up and down and up and down. Like gerbils with hormones. So, indeed, the dances equaled sweat smell. Wearing a breathing mask was discussed with mild sincerity on more than one occasion by teachers that I knew.

Having made your scent, to add to the memory, you'd also have to add in the sounds of the school; bells, kids yelling before, after, and sometimes during school; and the sound of teachers' voices—adult voices, through walls, at a distance.

In a well-managed school, after the bell rings and classes are underway, within minutes of the beginning of a period the only sounds you hear outside the office are adult teacher voices. Three minutes into the period, people are setting goals for the day, starting their concept introduction, getting to work. So you hear their voices, through the walls of your own room, if you have loud neighbors. I taught next to a math teacher once who had an Xman-like ability to project his voice through solid matter. His was the one voice I taught next to that was rarely muffled. He was a barker, emphasizing random words in each sentence.

"EIGHTH grade! COME on. You know better." Pause. "So HERE, we have the root. WHICH is what? That's (muffled). When (muffled, muffled.) So NOW, you need to (muffled) because that what you do with the result. JAMES! Eyes on me. That's RIGHT." Pause. "So now you need (muffled muffled)."

Mostly I'd hear their voices in a low murmur, like the sea, on either side of my room. Over the course of the year, it got to the point where you could even guess what they were saying at different times of day. When I was in the science office, and my earth science co-teacher was leading a class we didn't have together on the other side of the wall, I knew what part of his routine he was in by the cadence of the sounds. That was also a result of teaching with someone for six years.

Sometimes, in my room between classes, I'd hear kid laughter coming through the walls. Rarely, a kid yelling, freaking out. Then the low rumbles of the AP and the behavior specialist, talking some poor distraught kid off whatever emotional ledge they had climbed out onto.

Other times, as I walked down the halls and passed each open door I'd get an audio sample of whatever was happening in each room. Step, step. "The vacuole is the part of the cell..." Step, step, step, step, step. "So what makes a good thesis statement?" Step, step, step, step, step. "George Washington? Seriously? (Laughter) In fact, he was not the King of England..." Close to 800 people. Only 48 talking. That's what early in a period sounded like.

But the sound I think of most when I think of school is a slamming locker.

The locker is the epicenter of a kid's life In the Building. It contains what Vietnam vet and writer Tim O'Brien would term The Things They Carried. Their books, of course, but also piles of old graded papers, forms that were supposed to go home, pictures of their friends, their girlfriends, their cousins, pop stars, happy meal toys, Magic The Gathering cards, music in various forms, cosmetics, their friend's books, torn-up notebooks, all the detritus of their lives, duties and obligations between 7:50 a.m. and 2:12 p.m. every day. So when they had a chance, in those wonderful few minutes that followed every school day, when At Last It Was Over, they slammed the door on that day with authority.

A typical school locker is a steel box approximately 12 inches across and 30 inches high. If you slam that door, it makes a brassy, ringing clash, kind of like the sound two metal footlockers might make if you dropped them one on top of another. Because there is momentum, and the door is attached, there is also a brief period of reverb, after the door slams, lasting maybe half a second.

At 2:00 p.m., when the last bell rang, the kids poured out into the hallway to get their coats and backpacks. The last room I taught in had a short connecting hallway that led to the main hall on one side of the building. It took about two seconds for the leading wave of kids to get down that hall and out into the main hall. Their voices were a babel of greeting, insult, denial, joy and just plain yelling as they were released from their sonic lockdown for the day.

By 2:00:45 I'd hear the first door. SLAM. Then two at once, SLAM SLAM—"Dang, boy you..." The bell curve kicked in, then I'd hear—SLAM-SL-SLAMSLAM-S-SL-SL-SLAM-SLAM-SL-SLAM-LAMSLAM—"What!   No!"—SLAMSLAMSLAM—"She,   uh-uh   I'm   gonna..."—SLAMSLAM. SLSLSLAM — SLAMLAMSLAM—SL—"Hey, where you..."—SLAMSLAM—AP calling, "Vee Vang! Yeah, Vee! Gotta talk to you...no, you'll make the bus, come here for a second!"—SLAMSLAMSLSLAM. SLAM. Beat, downside of the curve—SLAM. SLAM-SLAM—shuffling feet, someone running—SLAM. And they were gone.

One time I saw a mild-mannered kid I knew slamming the heck out of his locker door. I asked him why he had to do that. He showed me: after years of slamming, the edge of the door formed a gentle sine wave of low-grade steel. "Only way to get it closed," he said. SLAM.

On reflection, maybe the reason the sound had such power for me was that it also signified for me that another day was done. Punctuation for the actions, reactions and inactions that shaped my experience for one more school day. I made my way outside, threw my briefcase and textbooks in the car's back seat, and when I closed the door, it was also with authority. SLAM.

OCTOBER

I am drowning in the funding streams

In the center of any classroom, under the desks, surrounded by dropped pencils, bits of torn-off spiral notebook paper, Jolly Rancher wrappers and random bits of makeup application equipment, there was an invisible drain. Into this drain flowed, as we said in the business, the funding stream.

The kids in any classroom have their education paid for by different budgets. All are paid for—at least theoretically, as the winds of politics allow—by the state. All are also paid for (hopefully) by the school district budget. But then it gets complicated. Some kids, who are learning English, have an additional funding stream. Others, who have qualified through testing and evaluation-supported due process proving they have a educational disability, have additional support paid for by a special education funding stream. The equipment in the room, from smart boards (partnership grant from large technology corporation), laptops and LCD projectors (paid for by federal grants), and even people (one aide with a salary paid for by ELL, another paid for by Special Ed), visiting tutors paid for by another grant, sometimes even little plastic bits used to teach math (grants from large local company).

Working in corporate America, I understand the concept of the silo. People fight over whose budget is paying for who to do what, and whose project is being funded by who, but in business it never gets down to the degree of granularity you find in a school. I can't remember ever going to the supply cabinet to get a roll of tape marked Training Department. I can't ever remember anyone, either in the publishing world or the software world, ever watching over budgets the way that schools are looked over. Sometimes, when you spend grant money, you have to account for every dime, showing how it is all used. You have to demonstrate outcomes, and measure metrics, even though the sums you are granted might only be a few hundred dollars. This, when people are more than willing to entrust you with their children for seven hours.

Where this really plays out is in the sources of a teacher's technology. For example, a teacher has a group of computers in a corner, on which a piece of writing-assistance software in loaded, designed to help students write longer, more complex sentences. The teacher is getting great results. Then spring break comes, and over the break, the standard software load for the district's computers is changed. When the teacher returns, the writing program is gone. The teacher asks the building tech to put the writing program back on, but the tech doesn't have a copy, and is not allowed to install non-standard programs, since his work is paid for by a different funding stream.

The teacher asks someone from the grant initiative funding stream to come out and reinstall the software. It doesn't work. By coincidence, the same writing program is also being funded by another initiative, this one designed to help English Language Learners. The teacher has discovered this by accident, talking to a colleague next door. The other initiative's tech, from the other funding stream, comes out and is able to make it work.

But the building tech says that if anything else happens on the corner computers, officially speaking he won't be able to fix them, because they are no longer standard. The tech is not happy about this, but is getting directions from a central IT department.

So the funding streams swirl around, keeping the kids from using the same program they had before the break. By the way, between each of these events, at least three days pass, because with five classes a day and more than 100 students, fixing the computers is not the teacher's main focus. In the end, the kids get to use the program again, at least until something else happens. I believe everyone has good intentions, and don't think this was anyone's goal when they allotted all the different funds in the first place. But that's how it ends up working.

It seems like a warped sense of priorities. The accountability for the funds and the use of the adult resources is of more concern than the kids using the computers, and the writing software, to write better. No one was particularly happy about it: teachers, techs, or kids, and we all got a little dizzy, as the funding streams swirled us round and round.

Conferences

A t our school, conferences were a focal point for continuous experimentation. Everyone knew, combining educational research and gut instinct, that once you met a parent at conferences, all your interactions with both student and parent would be different afterwards. When the student spoke of you at home, you'd be a person, not just a name. If a relationship existed, and a teacher put higher demands on a student, or even corrected a student in pretty clear terms, the trust level at home would be higher. Conversely, if the relationship developed at the conference went bad, neither the student or the teacher was going to have an easy time of it.

The trick was getting the people responsible for a child's welfare to come. That group, by the way, could include relatives and connections as diverse as grandparents, guardians, aunts, foster parents, older siblings or unofficial adoptive parents. For simplicity's sake, I'll use the word parents throughout, but it really could have been any of the aforementioned. I'd need to check with my administrators of the time, but I think the attendance figure we had hovered around 20 percent, at best. There were a couple of groups that didn't come, ever. Parents of high-achieving kids and parents of kids whose struggles were extreme rarely came. Parents of kids who were "doing just fine" also rarely came.

So the people who showed up were those committed to try to help kids go from okay to good, or from not okay to okay. There were many exceptions over the years, but this was the pattern.

It was not for lack of cultural sensitivity on the part of the school, either. There were always translators available: Spanish, Hmong, Somali, and staff who could fill in when the parents couldn't. I once ended up translating French for a student who had just moved to St. Paul from West Africa. The staff who specialized in building and maintaining our school's relationship with the African-American community were always in attendance.

Over the years, we tried a variety of programs—from big school welcome address to small and intimate groups. We tried different patterns of available times: afternoon Tuesday 3 p.m.-6:30 p.m., then Wednesday 5:30 p.m.-8 p.m.; a full weekday, followed by a night conference from 6-8 p.m.; spreading the conferences out over two weeks, in case people were traveling.

For some reason, we just never got a huge turnout.

I loved conferences because I got to be the teacher who told parents their kids they were doing well. My students often struggled seriously in general ed classes that were not differentiated, so it was great for me to say that someone's reading was improving, or they were doing better at math. I always found something good to say, because there always was. Even when the conversation took the form of, "If he did the work, he would be getting more out of it." Once the parents saw the way my materials were set up, I often got better results.

I had the homework configured so a kid could do 10 math problems and meet standard, because they were a small set of problems testing concepts that truly demonstrated if they had the skill. It was all day-to-day. If a kid brought a good effort level to most days, they would learn. Often, I got better homework completion rates after I explained that to the responsible adult.

Mostly, I just liked meeting the parents. I saw people just like me: they cared about their kids and expected them to do well. The system as a whole was pretty mysterious to many parents: it was mysterious to me, and I worked there. In seven years, I met dozens of parents, working as hard as they could to do what was best for their kids, as they saw it. I only ever met one mom who was clearly trying to work the system, arguing for her son to have a disability so she could get extra money. The whole Lazy Poor Person riff you hear in right-wing popular media was simply not in evidence. I met people working as hard as they could, typically with two jobs, doing whatever they needed to do to get by. They were primarily working-class, some Southeast Asian, some white, others African-American or Somali, some Native American. I knew that because they showed up.

The spring conferences were great. When I had the portable outside the school, the spring air would blow in, and I would welcome parents to my little classroom behind the school. We'd sit down in chairs really too small for adult-sized posteriors and talk for a while. The backdrop to our conversation was swallow birdsong from the nests under the western doors of the school, or the honks of migrating geese out on the playing fields. Both the birds and the people knew summer was coming, and with it, change, both for the kids and for us.

Conferences also offered a chance to demystify some of the special ed paperwork I sent home to people. I explained that the IEPs were written like legal documents, that they were there for people's protection, and that they were difficult for all of us to understand. I had been on the other side of that table, so I knew there was really no good way to hear that your kid is struggling, that there is something wrong with them in the eyes of the system. In fact, for kids with and without disabilities, it is the system that is broken, in fundamental ways, but that's another story.

Some teachers complained about conferences, but they were among my favorite teaching experiences, and many of the conversations I had on those days, those few hours out of the year, changed everything for a kid all though my two years with them. Pretty good return for a little time spent after school and some ice cream in the common area.

Rooms

The classroom is the epicenter of a teacher's life. Items in the rooms, their layout, and the arrangement of space took on a cabalistic mojo any priest of Stonehenge would recognize in a heartbeat. The room was where I spent 90 percent of my time, and if I was lucky (and good) enough, it became a safe space to operate out of, the world I built for my kids, and a place where good things could happen.

Only the most senior and best-connected (politically) teachers got the same room year after year. In my school, teachers of core subjects (math, history, science) had the best chance to keep their rooms.

In my seven years of teaching I had seven rooms, three in the first year alone. Special Ed teachers tend to be jammed down back hallways, around corners, in random spaces; I had a room once that was actually a corner of another giant room that had once been a wood shop, separated off with file cabinets and curtains. I had a tiny room big enough for only nine kids. I had a room that once had been a darkroom, with a vent for allowing chemically-saturated air to escape. The vent had been closed up, but not well, so that in the winter the temperature in the room was so low I let the kids get their coats from their lockers before class.

For one glorious two-year period, I was outside in portables. I loved my portable. It was my little cabin in the woods, and I had three huge playing fields to use to help me regulate and manage the collective emotional states and movement needs of my jumping bean students. I had one reading student who could never sit still during his individual reading period, so I sent him off with a book, walking, out around the backstop halfway across the field. I could see him the whole time. Maybe he was reading, maybe not, but at least he was attempting it. Outside the walls of the school, we watched the geese land in the playing fields during the fall, we watched the snow drift to earth in winter, in the spring we'd garden, putting in plants I brought from home.

Kids complained in the winter, but I think they actually liked the place. They'd stumble in, stamp off the cold, and then we'd settle down to work. It was quieter than the boisterous halls of the main building, and I think my best years teaching were there, in part because of the versatility of the space.

A room is to a teacher what a kitchen is to a chef. Everything is exactly placed. I always used tables, and at the beginning of each year, I taped down a numbered index card in the center of each table, which I used for random calling and getting tables to compete against each other. Tables were also great for flexible seating—three kids together, sometimes two, placed carefully, sometimes a kid alone, but facing me, up close to the front. Keeping the peace.

I paid a lot of attention to flow. If all the kids were to stand up at the same time and go out, would they come into contact with each other? Were there places they'd congest or congregate that could prove troublesome? If a kid needed something, was there a clear route to the storage of books to read, pencils, folders? I had my kids use folders with all their work and leave them in the room, so they could not be lost. Could the kids find their own folders? Could they manage their own supplies?

Materials management is critical in a room. I used materials packets to provide a full set of portable, yet duplicable material for each subject, complete with a weekly and daily agenda. So if a kid didn't have the week's packet, they could take another from a clear plastic rack.

In practice, a kid might say, "I can't find my packet." I could point to the place they could get another. I did not need to move. If a kid asked, "What are we doing today?" I pointed to the day of the week in the packet. Limited motion, nonverbal direction, all from a stack of paper. After a while they'd just keep the packet, since forgetting it didn't get them out of any work.

So much about room arrangement was preserving line of sight. Teachers plan out their classrooms every bit as carefully as soldiers plan fields of fire. There can be no blind spots, no places where a kid can hide entirely, or even hide a part of their body (texting or note-passing areas). All parts of the room had to be visible from wherever I stood or sat, especially during reading.

The reading program had rotations, one small group up front working on skills and strategies; another group on computers doing individualized learning, and another in a reading area, with chairs and books. From the horseshoe table where I sat with the small groups, I had to have a clear line of sight to all parts of the room, even back into the reading area. I had to be able to see all the computer screens; in case kids were going places they should not, rather than using the reading software. The kids may have been identified as having learning disabilities, but when it came to switching screens and hiding windows I'd stack their skills up against programmers anywhere.

The walls were another resource at my disposal. I had posters showing reading group membership (Red, Green and Blue), so that as kids were rotating to their next groups, I could watch the room, and if a kid couldn't remember their group, I could simply point at the poster, without taking my eyes off the movement. My walls also held calendars of events (so kids knew what was coming next) and charts showing kids' progress towards their goals, which, when we reached them, we'd celebrate. It's a matter of preference. Some teachers choke their walls with artifacts, some with aphorisms; some walls are stark and bare.

A teacher's desk is the equivalent of a truck mechanic's large toolboxes. In my drawers at any given time I had pens, pencils, mechanical pencils, permanent markers, dry-erase markers, hall pass pads, tape (scotch and duct), band-aids, Kleenex, hand sanitizer, lots of scissors, mini dry erase boards, rubber bands, and a lot of forgotten and confiscated items. Everything in the desk had to be accessible in less than 15 seconds, and findable without dropping my eyes for more than a second.

Chefs talk about "mise en place"—everything in its place— so they can meet the demands for speed in a restaurant. Teachers have the same need to handle the flood of requests that come their way. To provide for all I planned, all the kids asked for I hadn't planned, and anything I might need to improvise and adapt in the moment, I needed a pretty robust system.

I became so attached to my room, my desk and the world I had created, that when I cleared the walls and emptied out my drawers after my last day of teaching, I felt like I was somehow suddenly homeless.

Played: Telling the truth (?)

The ethics of being "played" were complicated, and I mention them as an example of how the cultural overlays of the wider world do not always apply in middle school.

To understand how this worked in my school, you first have to understand the ethos of possession that applied for kids In the Building. It was more a matter of holding by force than holding by name. For example, if a kid brought something of value to school, say a very cool jacket, or a new phone, they were stating implicitly they intended to defend the phone, and that if someone succeeded in taking it, that was as much their fault as the person who took it. This expectation applied to teachers as well.

My second year, I had a student who was the only kid I ever felt a little afraid of, possibly an actual sociopath. The last I knew of him, years later, he was serving time in a juvenile detention center, on weapons possession charges, and he had clear gang affiliations. At the time I knew him, he was like a baby shark. Young, but still very dangerous. So I'll call him Jaws.

For the classroom store I used to run, I kept the candy in cardboard cylinders (made from old Slim Jim canisters) in a plastic tub, locked in a steel cabinet in a back corner of my room. One day, Jaws masterminded a break-in, forcing the lock and taking most of the items in the store. When I found out about the break-in, student sentiment was against the thief. They felt that because I had made an effort to lock the candy up, it was wrong to steal it.

At this point, the identity of the student who took the candy was still unconfirmed, but I had suspicions. Another student, an extraordinary kid who pulled himself up from his bootstraps to such an extent that between seventh grade— when he arrived in my class at a second grade reading level— and eighth grade he did such good work he was nominated for the National Junior Honor Society, approached me very discreetly, after school in a side hallway. I'll call him E. He was a Walker, which meant he didn't have to leave right away with all the buses, so there were very few other kids in school to notice he was talking to me. E. said he wanted to tell me the name of the kid who had taken the candy.

This gave me serious pause. If he told me, I had to act on the information, but do it in such a way that no one could ever know E. told me, because an informer was universally despised, and I didn't want to put him in a bad situation. I also knew I had to send a message to the thief.

I asked E., are you sure you want to tell me? He gave me the name and the story. What Jaws had done was bully and cajole another kid, who had a serious case of bad-ass hero worship (villain worship?) for Jaws, into doing the hands-on work of opening the cabinet. That way Jaws could say he was not actually the one who forced the lock. The flaw in his master plan was that he did it in full view of the rest of the class, relying on his terrifying power to keep the kids silent. Except for E., who apparently was born with the courage of a lion. So I took the name, thought about it, and decided to make an announcement.

The next day, I said I was going to find out who had taken the candy, but until then I couldn't really have Store. How could I do that, I explained, when someone in here had taken stuff from me? The message was, of course, I couldn't let myself get played that way. That made the kids angry with the thieves. I watched, sidelong, the hero-worship kid, who was getting to the point in his own logic where he realized maybe doing this thing had been a Bad Idea. Jaws said nothing, just looked at me with his flat shark eyes. It wasn't with a lack of comprehension. He was actually pretty bright, and often did A/B work in my class when he was not out of the school system entirely for days on end. He was just assessing the situation in his own special way, which often reminded me of how a predator might look at a small animal it was about to eat.

I announced that the APs had some footage, shot from the hallway cameras, of two boys rushing out of my classroom with something in their hands. (The reality: the thieves had actually run into the classroom early, knowing I'd be coming over from another part of the building, had forced the lock, grabbed candy in front of their classmates, then left quickly and stuffed the candy in one of their lockers.) What I was saying was possible, but no such footage existed.

I told them that from the film, we could see who the boys likely were, but we had to get a really close-up look at what was in their hands to prove it. If, of course, anyone wanted to admit they did it, to myself or Mr. C. (the AP), they could and the consequences would be lessened. I knew the boys would not offer up their guilt. They were stealing from a teacher, which had serious consequences.

So I went to Mr. C. and told him what had happened. We decided to wait a week or so to pretend the video analysis was going on. When the time came for Store that week, the kids asked half-heartedly if we were still going to have it, but I was able, without too much feigned anger (it did actually piss me off) to say, you're joking right? When they saw I was holding the line on not having Store, they knew I'd also be pursuing the video angle. There was always footage of kids in the hall, but it didn't mean we could see anything. So we weren't lying either.

Finally, Mr. C. came in and got Jaws and his accomplice. He brought them into his office, said the video showed the two of them doing something, and asked them if they wanted to tell him what happened. Surprisingly, it was Jaws who offered up the fact he had done it. A little surprised, Mr. C. asked why. Jaws said because "the lock Mr. A had on that door wasn't nothin'." Mr. A. wasn't serious, he said, so we took the candy. In his mind I had locked it up, but not seriously, so I couldn't actually mind that much. E. was thereby spared the extreme danger of snitching on Jaws, by Jaws himself. That would hardly have been survivable. Instead Jaws added to his legend, to his hallway cred, by just offering up that he had done it and taking the hit for the other kid. Jaws got a three-day suspension, which I accepted without asking for further consequences (like criminal charges). E. was also able to survive. This is how a moral crisis is handled in the smelly, noisy halls of middle school.

If I hadn't locked the candy up, but instead relied on the honor system and loudly announced that the candy was in the back of the room, but I trusted the kids to be on their best behavior, even the most rule-oriented student in the room would have laughed. In that case, the thought process would be, Mr. A. is not even serious, so if we take the candy, that's on him. I would be allowing myself to be played. It'd be on me for being so naïve.

The same held true of the concept of telling the truth. For the kids, there were really three forms of truth. What Was True, What Was False and What You Could Get Away With.

At first this didn't make sense to me, and I was very rigid. When it turned out some kids I thought I knew well were less than truthful, had played me, I was disappointed until I ran one of the scenarios by T., my buddy and a very streetwise teacher.

He said, "Dude, that's on you. You have to be sure they can't even begin to play you. That's how they know you don't mess around." For kids with very little money, or in outright poverty, the system is not on their side. They are typically looking at an uncertain future; the road to middle-class prosperity is tough at best for the most resilient, for others they might be looking at another generation of fighting to stay alive in a world of hourly work and scarce resources. So the belief evolves that the system is too much to fight

310: IN THE BUILDING

completely, but if you can work it a little, that's ok.

As a teacher, you didn't want to be the hard-ass who never believed anyone, because at that point the kids wouldn't lie to you, but neither would they talk to you at all if they didn't have to. Then you couldn't connect and wouldn't get as much learning out of them. I knew a couple of teachers who ran their classrooms like that, and although there was discipline and rigor, they weren't a fun place to be.

Some teachers didn't understand the relativistic truth code and criticized its morals. I thought of it simply as the water the kids swam in–it was what it was–and unless I had a magic wand that changed socio-economic inequality on earth, I was going to stop thinking about it.

The converse was a classroom where a teacher was cloaked in the well-meaning, rosy glow of the belief that they were Here To Help The Downtrodden and believed everything the kids said, because they were Victims of Circumstance. The kids played teachers with this worldview like a violin, if not a whole orchestra. These teachers were often first-years, or AmeriCorps volunteers, and they very quickly wised up or left, disappointed somehow.

The bottom line on being played was simple. The kids, above all, were kids, and any 13- or 14-year-old anywhere— not just at my school—is hard-wired to find out what they can get away with. As an adult in that world, you simply had to build a structure in which the truth was visible.

Here's an example: for the majority of the time I was In The Building, there was no clear policy about how many times a kid could go to the bathroom. As a result, some teachers let kids go all the time; others never let them go. In the Never Let Them Go scenario, I'd end up with kids showing up in my early afternoon classes who could barely sit still. I wanted to give them an option, but neither did I want to get played.

So I told them they had a few minutes to get to the bathroom during passing time if they really needed to go. However, stuff happened. Maybe they were sick, or just hadn't gotten around to it. Therefore, they were allowed one bathroom visit per week. They couldn't save them up from week to week if they did not use them, by the way. (The kind of exploratory question a kid might ask, and one reason why my Clipboard of All Things took on the significance of a religious relic to me, scribbled with arcane notions and odd notes. It had a sheet for every week. By the time half the year had gone by, I would actually lock it in my car, since I literally would have lost critical records if I couldn't find it.)

On my Clipboard of All Things, I'd keep track. Of everything. I had a list of all the kids' names, and all the tasks we did in class. It was my external memory. So, when a kid had gone to the bathroom that week, I'd make a mark. Early on, at least one kid would try to go twice. I'd tell them, nope, you went already, and show them the mark. It was an in-between approach—neither draconian nor lenient, the sweet spot where I tried to operate all the time.

I was definitely soft-hearted compared to some, but I remembered being a kid, trapped in the system, desperate, and I knew that as a kid in that state, I wasn't learning anything. So I'd rather be a little soft-hearted, as long as things didn't go haywire.

Occasionally, clever girl students would try to cash in on their monthly cycle. I'd give them some leeway, and then make a very discreet mark on the clipboard. Not something you want to leave a written record of. But enough so that 10 days later, when they asked again, I'd tell them, "Nice try, but I have a daughter and a wife, so I know what you are saying basically isn't biologically possible." They usually didn't try again. For most kids, that was where the line was drawn.

There were still rare cases of teachers having things stolen from their desks or from unlocked cabinets. And while I did not think that was right, after a few years, I have to admit a small part of me thought, "What were you thinking, leaving that in there unlocked? You got played."

Dances

A lot of my colleagues thought I was crazy to enjoy the dances, but I did. They were held in the daytime, between 12:30 p.m. and 2 p.m., about six times a year. To have a dance at our school at night, or one that kids from other schools could attend, would have been foolish. We needed to know exactly who was there, for the safety of everyone involved.

The dances were used as a carrot for good behavior, with the corresponding stick being time in the study hall when everyone else was having fun. This combination deterred some kids from crossing the line, but the kids that just couldn't manage to contain themselves rarely got to a dance at all. If they learned anything about the way actions connect to consequences from that, then it was worth the pain. I worked one of the study halls once, and was in a situation where I had to lean on a kid, and he pushed back, saying, "What are you going to do, keep me from going to the dance?"

The first dance of the year was like a debutante party: the seventh-graders were introduced socially to everyone else in the school, the eighth-graders could evaluate the new kids, and many patterns of social organization and power were formed. We as teachers got a chance to find out who might go off the chain completely, unable to regulate themselves even in the context of such a narrow event.

The excitement level building up to the dances was huge. As a uniform school, it was one of the only times our kids had a chance to show their true colors, literally. In the case of the Somali girls, those colors were myriad, and the many-hued radiance of their hijab made it look like butterflies had come to earth and were roaming the school. There was a lot of conversation, at times when that could happen, and shopping trips for new clothes, and girls getting their hair done for the day by aunts, moms and cousins.

The time of great preparation happened for most of the dances, but for the Valentine's Day dance, when relationships had been established and the stakes were incredibly high, it reached reality-TV proportions. Into the mix, throw the total angst of non-proficient, romantically-inclined kids, and the fact that hormones were in high-grade overdrive, and the Valentine's Day dance prep was epic.

The dances happened on what we called an Early Release Day schedule. This meant shortened classes, and kids decked out in their finery all day long. I knew, especially on Valentine's Day, not to expect much academically. They'd roll out of the buses, boys slightly ill at ease, yet proud, in clothes ranging from Goth to business suit; girls with their hair done, some in prom dresses, others teetering on older sisters' high heels. By the time the dance actually happened, some of the high-heeled girls had terrible blisters, but bravely bore the pain. I always kept some clear Band-Aids around for dance days.

Kids who knew they weren't going to be able to attend,

as a consequence of prior behaviors, often found ways for themselves to be removed from the equation. It was very typical, by the time the dances happened, for them to have been sent home on that day.

When it was finally time for the big event, the kids went to their homerooms, then the principal called the kids to the gym by classroom. Releasing a giant horde of middle-schoolers, amped up beyond reason, dying to be free to access both the opposite sex and video games, all at once, would have been like the run for lifeboats on the Titanic.

Any teachers who didn't have a homeroom, including me, would grab some lunch, sit and wait until there were enough kids in the gym, then go to our assignments. Every teacher had a station during the dance. The most proficient at behavior management or teachers studying to be principals got the study halls. The best assignment of all was the movie, shown in the auditorium. That job was typically given to long-tenured teachers. Some other teachers had specialty duties like taking tickets (usually counselors and social workers), but most of us had gym.

The upper gym at my school comfortably held three volleyball courts, the lower held a basketball court. Upper gym was where the games (video, ping-pong, board, and others) were held. There was also a photo booth, manned by volunteer teacher photographers, where kids could get pictures taken in their dance finery, or take snaps of couples holding hands. A lot of other behavior we normally would have cracked down on was in full display. We spent half the time, about 45 minutes of our shift, in the first gym location.

We'd stand and talk to other teachers, talk to kids, or whatever made sense to pass the time.

It was great, from my point of view. After continually shutting the kids down, keeping them silent, keeping them on task, it was great to watch them actually having fun—running around in circles with the energy level that only middle-schoolers really have, continuous movement for 90 minutes, literally without stopping.

Dances were often when I had my first real conversation with a kid, ones that would gravitate to me, maybe a kid that didn't reach out to other kids yet, and we would talk about video games or sports or whatever. It was at a dance I discovered that a kid I had in Algebra who could barely do simple equations had a really impressive knowledge of World War Two for a 13-year-old. It was in a corner upstairs by the ping-pong tables that I found out that a kid was brain injured, but the family had not told the school system, for fear of marginalization. Dances were, for me, one of the only times I could freely talk.

I counseled kids on relationships, if they asked. I made jokes I'd never make in the classroom, and for a lot of the kids, the Halloween dance was the first time I became a human being. I was pretty restrained for the first part of every year. I had a colleague who could be himself from Day One and never lose his hold on the classroom (being merely mortal, that didn't work for me). I just gradually thawed, opening up slowly, the days before Christmas typically the first time I let off and allowed the kids to run a little. If I did it before that, they would eat me alive and spit out the bones.

Nothing personal, but that was the way it was.

Downstairs at a dance, though, was a different matter. After 45 minutes I'd head downstairs to the gym, which by that point was like a giant dryer filled with wet towels that smelled of Axe, middle school perfume, and sweat. Into that humid mist, place a DJ—usually someone's uncle—flashing lights and the latest hip hop, cranked up just louder than the highest decibel level the principal preferred.

The kids moved in a kind of Brownian motion; ebb, flow, clump. Individuals, packs, round and round. Some danced, some watched, some attempted to find corners where no teachers could see them, but that didn't work since there were typically no less than 25 teachers in the room, so we had it pretty well covered.

Circles formed, brave young dancers would step in, bust a move, show their stuff, and step out. Bravado, wild abandon, grace, ineptitude, and controlled skill were on display. Circles formed around the proficient, and the less proficient watched in awe. One of my colleagues actually could break dance, so the kids loved it when he stepped in.

Packs of girls ran around chased by a single annoying brave boy. A single girl fled a pack of seventh-grade boys trying to talk to her. Some of the Hmong kids formed full family units, boyfriends and girlfriends proudly—yet self-consciously—holding hands. The Somali girls flowed like wisps of color through the darkness.

Always, by about an hour into the dance, a girl sat in the corner, sobbing. She would just have broken up with her boyfriend, her friends consoling her, typically glaring at the guy, who would also typically be somewhere in the near distance putting on a brave face, his friends around him. The boys: "Ain't nothing dude, you're single now." The girls: "He's such a player. You're better off without him." Micro-divorce court, hopefully not a vision of things to come.

The songs surged and thumped, the kids spun and spun, and after about an hour and fifteen minutes, even the middle school energy level would start to drain off, unable to sustain itself, despite its nuclear half-life power. Kids would start to slow down, even sit.

The dance was drawing to a close.

By this time even I was done, my senses assaulted and drained, and though I was happy for the kids, I was ready to go home. I tried to record the sounds of a dance once on my phone. It sounded like a combination of a heavy ocean shorebreak and hip hop radio.

Two o'clock came, the music stopped and the kids shuffled up the stairs. For once, they had met an event that matched and drawn out all their energy. Kids grabbed their coats, slammed their lockers and headed out.

The silence was deafening.

NOVEMBER

Voices

Classrooms are filled with tables, chairs, stools, chalkboards, whiteboards and Smart boards. Books, worksheets, pencils and pens litter every flat surface. Clocks, bells and schedule posters tell time. But the single greatest tool

I did it, like an opera singer, bracing my chest and neck, pushing from my stomach, choosing every word like a diamond cutter working on a flawed but beautiful gem. Eyes scanning the classroom for hands working in acceptable patterns, thinking one sentence ahead, my speech on a delay loop, like a radio station broadcasting knowledge. any teacher has in their arsenal is their voice. Voice is the wind and weather in a classroom. It is ritual, cant, chastisement, encouragement, and illumination. Above all, it is not a natural conversational voice.

I'm a soft-spoken guy, and people who never saw me work

can't imagine me projecting enough to cover a full-sized science classroom with 30 eighth-grade boys in it. But

To understand why teacher voices are so intentional, imagine you're seeing through a teacher's eyes as they speak. Your mind is simultaneously processing what you need to say next, how you'll say it clearly without sacrificing expectation in your vocabulary (yet not losing kids), how you'll lead into a new concept as cleanly as possible. You watch yourself as you speak, framing a question to build on basic knowledge, calling a single kid back to focus, then pushing on to higher order thinking. Leading the dialog, to a question, with a nudge (not too easy), bump and bridge to other kids, use a kid's response to hold the class, scan for listening eyes, affirm, reinforce, switch. You raise your voice for emphasis, pause, affirm, make a joke for the kids (not too many, that's Teacher Boring), make a joke for yourself (that's Teacher Self-Amusement, which everyone does sometimes.)

Anger is another register in teacher voice. Miss S. (all women teachers, when speaking, were called Miss "Lastname", whether married or not), an English teacher who started the same year as me, was very intentional about her anger. She told me once she saved it for at least a month in, and used it really visibly to set a bar. I saw teachers who got angry all the time, in which case it became background noise, and teachers who never got angry, in which case the kids stopped worrying that they would, which then became a lost advantage.

When you do get angry, you have to be really, really careful how you frame it. As your voice goes up in volume, every kid is listening, parsing your words like a defense attorney, waiting for any kind of slip. "He said ___ " could equal Career Done. Whenever I raised my voice, which was very rare, I felt both the anger and the caution, holding it, calibrating it like the rods in a nuclear reactor, controlled burn, manmade fire.

If you can't control your temper, if the kids know they can get you to lose it, they are on you like sharks in bloody water. They know they can gain control of the classroom that way, that your anger overcomes any of theirs 10 times over. The kids, of course, can say basically anything they want, albeit with consequences. But we could not.

The way in which you use your voice, the sound most often heard in a classroom, the channel, the medium, justice system, support system, comic relief, self-amusement, and all the other modes of communication a teacher's voice serves, is tricky when done perfectly, catastrophic when done poorly, nuanced and complex and ever-changing, tiring and exhilarating.

Just like the job itself.

Due process

When I first decided to enter the classroom, I wanted to be a social studies teacher. I love history, have a master's in political science, and have a significant appetite for information relating to the world of people and cultures, the world we build with our ideas and imperfections alike.

But two funny (?) things happened on the way to AP US History. In my very first class, an overall survey of education and society, there was a lecture on special education. The teacher who presented was an adjunct instructor, a working teacher, and very proud of what she did. Like most people, before I knew better, I thought special ed was something that happened in a school's back building, where people took care of kids in helmets and wheelchairs, and it wasn't really school.

But she talked about PL 94-142, The Education for All Handicapped Children Act of 1975 (EHA). She told us how special ed was actually a civil right and shared with us the story of the long fight for rights to equal education. My underdog radar kicked in when she talked about how special ed teachers are advocates for kids in a system that is not designed for difference, and that the kids and teachers both had federal law on their side.

I thought, sure, I can probably take a bunch of middle-class suburban kids from third base to home, but these special ed kids, maybe they weren't even allowed to get up to bat, and I could be a part of changing that.

The second event was that as part of that same course, I was required to log classroom observation hours, and ended up at an elementary school near my house, where I sat watching some kids who had been pulled from the mainstream and stuffed in a small room in the back of the school, and how hard the teacher fought to get them to the same place as everyone else.

I was hooked. So I changed my major to teaching kids with learning disabilities, and spent the next two years learning about all the myriad ways a kid's mind can rebel, challenge and struggle, keeping them from rolling smoothly down the rails of the mainstream school system. I found how they could get support—in reading, writing, math and social skills—and first glimpsed the maze-like world of regulations and paperwork that ensure their access to these services.

Later, as a tenured teacher, I wished I could go back and tell my professors that due process was the one thing they didn't prepare me for. I went to a really outstanding program, and felt like I hit the ground running in every area but one— the creation and management of Individual Education Plans. In that case, the ground hit me, repeatedly. We had a class where we wrote one IEP. It took two months, and there were four of us. That's the equivalent of having a single bullet fired at you in basic training and believing you are ready for actual combat.

Briefly, an IEP outlines the reasons a child qualifies for special ed services. They can be many: from reading only, to math, to both; to significant social and behavioral troubles; to purely physical reasons, ranging from asthma to multiple severe disabilities.

The context for these, and the window through which they are viewed, is how they impact a kid's ability to go to school. The world outside may present different challenges, but the IEP is there for school, a document to blueprint the correct degree of assistance that allows them to stay, as closely as possible, in the least restrictive environment where they can learn.

Writing IEPs is a major undertaking. There are several large sections, and the wording in them has to be exact. For the first few years I was teaching, we had a compliance officer, who read IEPs day-in day-out, then returned them where there were mistakes or corrections. I dreaded seeing the green IEP folders in my school mailbox because it meant the work I did was coming back to me again, for more work. Because the laws and how they were enforced was always changing, even when I had done it for years, there were always changes to make. A short IEP was eight to nine pages long, and I had many that ran 13 to 14 pages or more.

The assessment process, a much longer undertaking, establishes exactly why a kid needs assistance. From the results of the assessment, we had to create several kinds of goals, and indicate the exact amount of time each week a kid needed to be with teachers and specialists who could help them meet these goals. The goals had to be exact, including minutes they spent with each specialist each week, down to which quantity of digits they could add and subtract (but not multiply and divide), and what a teacher would do to ensure a kid could meet these goals by the time an academic year had passed.

At first I thought I had to try to achieve every single goal in an IEP, and lost a lot of sleep. Over time, as I did them again and again (by way of reference, my first year I only had 15 to do, by my last year my caseload was 25) I started to realize that everyone was much more concerned with whether they were done on time, and all the t's were crossed and i's dotted, than whether they were literally an exact guide to teaching a kid.

The reality was, for most of the kids, the goals were similar. They needed to work on reading faster, more fluently, and with greater comprehension. In math they needed to reinforce basics, be able to finish problems with correct answers, and build up their foundation for higher math concepts.

Other kids needed to work on transition, which was a plan to help a kid get where they wanted to go in life. To do this, we filled out a questionnaire that assessed life skills, and awareness of the world, and plans for the future.

It was often pretty funny, since the questions were designed for high school kids, but for a variety of procedural reasons we were required to have them finished before a kid got to high school. After questions like, "Can you take the bus?" or, "Where did you go on your last family vacation?" (Often they had never been on one), there were questions like, "Do you read the newspaper?" (YouTube?), or "What would you like to be doing 10 years from now?" My favorite answer to that question was from a seventh-grader, a very sharp kid. He looked me straight in the eye and said, "How am I supposed to know that? I'm 12 years old."

The other part of due process that made it so involved was that every three years, a kid had to get reevaluated, to see if they still qualified for and needed special ed services. To me this was quite reasonable, as it allowed an exit from the stigma (good) and support (also good, because it meant they were independent) of the program and into the wider world. We did a battery of tests to be sure they still faced the same academic challenges they had when they were first identified.

Typically we administered the Woodcock-Johnson III, an academic test that scaled up from simple to more complex problems. A kid kept going until they incorrectly answered six questions in a row, then that section was complete.

For example, in the math calculation test, the first problem was 2+2, and 22 questions later, the questions covered high school trigonometry. Reading and word identification worked the same way. The words started simple, and got harder. I only had one kid ever make it into the high school realm. On the WJ-III, as we called it in the trade, there were a variety of subtests: Word ID, Fluency, Basic Math, Math Fluency, Reading Comprehension, Sentence Writing, and so on. There was a critical mass of tests you were required to give to provide a fair account of a kid's academic and cognitive landscape.

Most of the kids I worked with, and over the years there were dozens, showed clearly why they needed specific strategies to work on their academic skills. They simply did not have them yet. Most of them also had become experts at what the kids called "frontin'"—in other words, camouflaging their lack of skills.

The test was administered one-on-one, in a quiet space, and there were time limits on some parts of the test. I often did the test for other teachers, for example, the Emotional and Behavioral Disorder specialists, who didn't have as much training in interpreting the academic results. In large part, I found even the most agitated, chair-throwing kid to be a calm and willing participant when we were working together. They always asked, "How did I do?" I told them they were getting better all the time, which was universally true. It was just a matter of how fast.

The most tragic administration I ever did was for a kid from the EBD program, an extremely withdrawn seventh grader. She had to have a female aide in the room as I gave the test because she was unable to be alone in a room with any male. We had to get the test done to remain in compliance, so against all the rules, I asked the aide to stay in, otherwise there was no way the girl was going to be able to get it done. The only thing the girl said, other than to give her answers and say hello, was "Keep the door open. Please." I gave her the test and tried not to let her see I felt like crying.

Administering the test took up the better part of two lunchtime preps (two hours at least), so the timing of how I set up test administration, then writing up the results, before I actually met with a parent, was critical, since I only had one prep a day. It took about two hours to write up the test, over and above all the other things we were doing as teachers.

There was a busy season for due process, typically between late January and early April. Then, depending on my caseload, I could be doing three to five IEP meetings a month, and also at least one Evaluation Summary Report (re-evaluations for eligibility). All of these had to be scheduled, and that was a feat of organization comparable to the D-Day invasion.

First of all, I had to track how many times I reached out to the family and tried to schedule the meeting. Typically, I made two phone calls and wrote a letter. In the case of people speaking a language other than English, I also had to get some time from the translators, most often Spanish and Hmong, who were trained in the exact terminology of special ed in each respective language. Then I had to schedule the meeting at a time when both the parent and myself could come (and the translator, if required.) I also had to ask a colleague to be there, to serve as a "district representative," someone who could verify my results to ensure consistency and validity to the conclusions I drew. There also had to be an admin representative, typically the AP. That was just for an IEP. If anyone else was involved, doing another evaluative test, they had to be at the meeting also.

So a typical ESR meeting required scheduling between three and five adults, and many ESRs could include more people, after inviting other specialists. In a busy month, that meant arranging for at least 30 individual calendar events with people. I was also serving as district rep for other people, so add in a few more meetings. Once again, over and above three preps and grading.

The result was we basically had two full-time jobs—one as a teacher; the other as a quasi-psychometrician, social worker and low-level bureaucrat. The strain this put on people was vast. It showed once a week, when we had our meeting with the department chair and went over the assessments in progress. The meeting was called Child Study, and it took on the rapid-fire exchanges of Aaron Sorkin dialogue. The kids to be assessed comprised a huge list. Their names would come up, and despite the overload, people just kept volunteering to help each other.

Department Chair: "Where are we at with x? That's an EBD re-eval, right?"

Case Manager (EBD teacher) "Yup. Also LD. Been trying to get in touch with Mom, no luck so far. He needs a Woodcock."

Learning Disabilities teacher #1: "I'll do that." (LD teachers helped the EBD teachers do academic tests.)

LD teacher #2: "How many you got?"

LD teacher #1: "I'm not bad right now, I have two in March, I can do that before we get there."

LD teacher #2. "Thanks, I'm buried right now. I have three this month."

Department Chair: "OK so 360 (district HQ) wants us to add a new document to all the IEPs, called the Record of Reasons for Non-Attendance. There's been a lawsuit. Details to come."

Silence. For me, adding a new form meant adding 25 more line items to include in my process. Also, we have to document why people aren't there at the meetings? We already contact them, and often they don't come. So if they don't respond in the first place, and they don't come, how can we find out why they didn't come?

More silence.

Department Chair: "Ok, so, moving on, we're getting ready for the Office of Civil Rights audit…"

The water rose and rose, but somehow the levee never broke. Because for the kids' sake, we just kept piling on the sandbags.

Gangs

We talked about them a lot, and there was certainly evidence they existed in our school, but I was never sure how much of that was real, versus how much of it was part of our pride at working at a school that was Not Like The Others. Part of our, I'm An Urban Teacher And I Know About Gangs and You Don't kind of thing. How much we really knew was debatable.

One year a police unit that specialized in gangs came and presented for us at professional development, so we would know what signs to look for. They gave us a breakdown on international gangs (like the Mexican drug gangs that have local branches in most cities); nations and their affiliations (East-West); national gangs like the Crips and the Bloods, regional powerhouse gangs like the Vice Lords (a Chicago institution that reached out into Minnesota) then strictly local gangs. We also learned the distinctions between a gang and a set or clique, which was kids who were basically friends but also did some low-level criminal activities together.

One of the fascinating things about Minnesota gangs is that sometimes, since there were so few minorities, even historically ethnic gangs (African-American or Latino) would take in white members. They had a staffing problem, I guess.

It was all quite interesting, and for a while afterwards I think we saw gangbangers under every rock. It did help us in enforcing rules, such as no gang symbols written on folders, and the like. For some mysterious reason the Gangster Disciples use a Star of David, which made me laugh internally when I thought of some pious kid in St. Louis Park (a neighborhood with a large Jewish population in the Twin Cites) being hauled into the principal's office because he had written a gang symbol on his folder. But we were not entirely paranoid, there were traces of activity, and there was recruiting going on.

You'd see kids doing a quick furtive hand gesture at a distance down the hall, a handshake, but only part of it, not something you could really report. Or did you see it? Kids wrote things on their folders and didn't truly know what it meant. I had one girl in a class I was covering as a sub tell me adamantly that she was "not gonna use red, un-uh, no way" to highlight something. I looked at her and said "You really want to have that conversation with me? Or with an Assistant Principal? Is it really worth representing like that?" The reason being, of course, that she wanted everyone to know she was a Crip, or think she was.

Most of the activity was "wannabe"—kids who felt vulnerable, wanted power, wanted to be someone. I had a kid whose life ambition was to be in the Latin Kings. He wrote it all over his folders, even when he got suspended. He came to school stoned a couple of times, and was stunned that I had recognized what that looked like. (I had seen it in movies, of course). After he had been suspended, they found not just pot in his locker but gang-related stuff. It was like the way some kids always know they want to be Marines. He ended up actually being in the Latin Kings, I found out later, so at least I give him credit for following up on his long-term life goals.

Sometimes there were tragedies related to wannabe-ism. One year a group of very dangerous kids convinced another kid who was emotionally vulnerable, and not the sharpest knife in the drawer, that they were actually Gangster Disciples, and that they could jump him in. (Jumping someone in is basically beating him or her up, one way to be initiated into a gang.) This kid believed gang membership would protect him when he was in high school. They beat the kid up pretty badly, and of course, they were not in a gang, just jackasses. Fortunately they were not very careful, some of it was caught on camera, and they were all suspended.

The reason everyone was worried about it all was if gang symbols were represented at school, and other kids were actually in gangs or aspiring to be in gangs, they automatically had to retaliate. If an affront was made, it had to be immediately answered, so it was the collateral damage from gang activity everyone wanted to avoid. There were few gang-related fights at school, and interestingly, they were mostly girls, and those were vicious. Mostly, it was a lot of talk.

We also wanted to be able to steer kids clear of gangs if they were willing to listen. There were a couple of people who were respected enough to do that, and if they could, they did, since typically the gang life leads to a kid being dead, disabled or in prison. Not many Original Gangsters both make it past 30 and live outside the justice system.

We had a kid once in science who was the real deal,

though. He was tall, maybe 6' 2", good-looking, and ran part of the school like it was a private fiefdom. He was very, very smart, and ruthless.

Everyone knew what he was up to, but he was clever, always using cutouts and having people do things for him. Even his homework. I asked once, so where's your homework? He smiled at me, a little chilling: "Man, you kidding, I don't do that, got people that do that for me." We watched him after that, but the work was always in his own handwriting. Other kids did the research, he'd copy it, then read it. He could always answer any questions we asked, so there was no way to prove anything.

He wanted us to know he was cheating, challenged us to catch him, and we could not.

That same kid, on the Valley Fair field trip (last day of the school year, to an amusement park) made a point of changing into a t-shirt with his gang number airbrushed on it once we arrived. Knowing, with the instinct of a reef shark hunting, that at Valley Fair he was off school property, there was no dress code that day, and that as long as he got off the bus and stepped directly out into the street, we could not do anything.

One time I had to do a presentation about the school website. It was not exciting material, and for some reason I was inspired to create a presentation describing us as a gang, the 310s. (That was our school number within the district.) Since we had just had the presentation from the cops, the timing was good. I went on about how you can recognize 310s (lanyard, colors of blue and gold, dry-erase marker stains on their fingers.) I said their main activity was dealing knowledge, and were often heavy users themselves. I said they typically hung out at the school, in the lounge or in hallways, but you could also apprehend them at Starbucks on the weekend, and they'd often be carrying large quantities of contraband papers they were grading.

It went over well. Some people even went so far us to make us a gang sign, arms crossed, three fingers on one hand displayed, five on the other side, opening and closing your hand twice.

We felt bad, silly, and a part of something at the same time. Jumped in, by our everyday lives at school.

I'm still proud to be a 310.

Pay attention

We were at PD once when a presenter pointed out we didn't need to worry about the kids paying attention. They're always paying attention. Just maybe not to us.

Imagine school from a kid's point of view. You walk in the door, maybe get some breakfast, maybe talk to a friend or two, then you go to homeroom, you get two more minutes to talk, do whatever you want, then the drumbeat begins.

"Good morning, need your attention up here." The homeroom teacher gathers the class's eyes up front. And so it begins, again and again, all day long, you are being asked for your attention, attention, attention. Granted, there are many parts of the day when you grant your attention, when something is happening that you are interested in. But for the majority of the time, at least from the point of view of your teachers, you are not paying attention.

Every lesson has a beginning, an anticipatory set, in teacherese. A teacher sets the stage for the day. It could be a recap of the day before, it could be some kind of demonstration, it could just be a teacher outlining what you are doing that day. The teacher wants you to know, so you know stay engaged that hour. Maybe you hear it, and maybe you don't. So 25 minutes later, when you switch from lecture to lab groups, and you go, what are we doing? You get a Teacher Look that means—Weren't you paying attention?

In a perfect world, teachers wish students were paying attention at all times, like dogs watching someone with a ball in their hands, getting ready to throw. You know, as the student, that you are not doing this.

You also know there are degrees of attention. The most foolhardy, the ones who really don't care anymore, demonstrate a total lack of attention. You can tell because you even have teachers that tell you what it looks like. Attention is "Eyes on me, one voice at a time, facing forward." Some teachers just say they know it when they see it. Which means they don't.

Some kids draw, doodling on pieces of paper. The disadvantage of drawing is that the teacher knows how long it takes to draw certain things. Like, for example, if your friend has drawn a really cool manga image over the course of the class, the teacher will see it when they come around to check the work, especially if they are observant, and know you had to have had a blank page when the class started. But not all teachers notice that. If they don't, you say you drew it at home last night. They might not be able to prove it, but afterward they will be watching for you, looking to see if you are drawing. If you draw pictures of whatever is getting studied, many times you can get away with lots of drawing, especially if you learned from some elementary teacher to say that you are a visual learner. Thus gets you at least 10 minutes of non-attention time every class, once the teacher thinks you are drawing diagrams, when in fact you are just drawing whatever.

Playing with bits of papers and pens, with stuff on the

front of your binder, is not a bad option. As you do it, if the teacher calls you on it, you can always claim you were listening. It's hard for a teacher to prove you weren't, even though you both know you weren't. "I was listening," can get a follow-up statement: "That's good, but eyes up here."

The plastic sleeve on the front of a three-ring binder is another good way to spend time. You can poke holes in the plastic, you can pull on it, and you can insert paperclips into the sides. It ends up looking like a barista's ears.

The ninja masters of middle-school paying attention, though, are the kids who can look up front, eyes on the teacher, facing forward, and have absolutely no intention of absorbing any information at all. They can face their heads forwards, in every way the picture of polite attentiveness, and this will go unnoticed, except in the rare and unfortunate occasion one of these ninja masters is asked a question during a time in deep trance state. Then, it is like the kid is coming up from under deep water, and as a fellow student you almost feel bad for them, at the depth of their exposure.

The kid will say "Wha....Wha...What was the question?" Usually the teacher has been in a rapid fire exchange, and has called on the kid as a mid-ranger (a kid likely to have the answer to a moderately hard question—not the kid who answers every question, but who answers some.) Many of these kids are among the best attention artists, but when they get busted the class will usually end up laughing.

The flip side of the attention scale is the kid who pays attention too much: to everything, in fact. The teacher definitely wants everyone's attention, but this kid is focused on anything and everything that happens in the classroom. While the teacher is talking, you see them looking at the teacher's shoes, at some girl playing with a comb, at the birds out in the field, and the new poster on the wall, at their own knee, at the clock, and you watch it building and building up in them, until finally, in response to a basic classroom question, the kid will just blow up.

The teacher will ask, "Can anyone tell me what usually goes with a verb? An adjective or an adverb?" and the kid will explode. "Adverb, but then why do you have new shoes on and how many minutes are left in class how many cans of food do you have to bring to the dance to get in for $5 and why did you drive a different car I saw you driving in when I got off the bus and it is your wife's car what does your wife do for a living and anyway why do we have to learn about this?"

Into the ringing silence that follows the teacher will typically blink a couple of times, answer one question, since the class is only 52 minutes; or answer no questions and just roll on. You don't know what the future might hold for this poor kid in high school. If you're lucky the explosion happens in 5th period, which makes the rest of the day interesting, and you only have one more period to go.

All day, the beat goes on:

"Afternoon eighth graders, focus up here please…"

"Before we break, look up here…"

"I'm holding my hand up, you know what that means…all hands up, please. Need your attention."

"You'll be done in 10 minutes…I already said that…weren't you paying attention?"

"Need your attention...."

"Eyes up here please..."

"Focus up front."

"Voices off."

"Need your attention..."

By the time you get on the bus after school, you don't have any attention left.

Prep

P eople have the impression that teachers just walk into a classroom, the bell rings and they start talking. After all, that's what happens in romantic comedies, when the attractive lead (either male in tweed jacket with elbow patches, which would be like wearing a wetsuit in my non-air-conditioned school) or female, impossibly lovely and energetic, as she faces cheery (or stereotypically blank-faced, gum-chewing) students, and after a quick embrace in the hallway, our Hero/Heroine runs in the door to teach. The love interest, of course, has no visitor's pass and has somehow managed to get into the center of a busy school and stand around in the hallway without any staff member in sight. But that's Hollywood.

Prep, in fact, is the iceberg that teaching is the tip of. Even if a teacher is responsible for only one subject (which was never the case for me) you still have a long list of things to get ready each day, and it goes way beyond making copies. As a preamble to this, what I'm about to describe was the way I prepped. Everyone does it differently. I also had some particular demands, namely the additional burden of special ed paperwork, which left me with less time, but most other teachers had additional responsibilities as well, so I was not unique in that lack of time.

Imagine I was teaching single-step equations in algebra.

First, I had to decide what to extract from the textbook. For example, in Algebra, I might decide to cover Chapter 2, Sections 1 and 2 that week. Then I gauged how fast we could get through that material. Textbook publishers (and this might have changed since schools started using iPads, but was still true when I was in the classroom) have a requirement. They need to sit down in a district boardroom somewhere and explain why each book costs $125. So they cram as many problems, activities, expanded teacher concept explanation, reading strategy reinforcement and standardized test support onto every page that is physically possible. If I did everything they put in there for each concept, I'd have needed an 18-hour school day and a 360-day school year.

So first I picked out the very small areas I would actually cover. Then, I figured out how I'd get my point across, in different creative ways. Trade secret: if you just stand up front and talk, also unlike in the movies, the kids will not magically just learn. If you build it, they may or may not come. So you have to make a way for them to learn (whatever it is) they may actually participate in. I looked through the week and talked to myself (out loud, it made me feel better and got me a better seat at Starbuck's as I worked late Sunday nights) "…maybe Monday I do the intro, Tuesday I review with a video, then application with a game, then a harder version of the same concept…then quiz." Unlike in much of the corporate learning I've been involved with, in a school it's critical for students to prove they are learning. So I'd work up a quiz for mid-week and a test for the end of the unit, crafted to match department, district, and national standards.

Then I started building the paperwork. Knowing that for my kids book management was a challenge akin to passing the CPA exam, and that finding a page in a big book was a golden opportunity to stall, I made packets out of copies of the textbook pages, carefully focused on what we were doing. The work of each day was labeled with the day of the week— Monday, 9/13/2012, and then I'd have a set of problems to be done for the day. As I did this, I had to allow for several factors. Early on, I used to only have one sheet for each day. Then I learned that for some of my kids, four problems were too many. For others, a school lifetime of feeling extreme pressure to "get the work done" led them to rapidly fill out the worksheet with a combination of correct and random answers. I had to have some extra pages for each day for them.

I started putting numbers on everything. My grading scale was: 2.0-Meets Standard, 3.0-Above Standard, 4.0-Beyond Standard. To get the kids motivated to do the Meets Standard, I'd pick between six and eight problems I knew covered the standard, then draw a line with a sharpie on the master page. To get a 2.0, they just had to do those problems. For 3.0, it was the same concept, except with decimals or fractions. I drew another line, for 4.0— the same concept, including word problems. Then I added another page called Extra, for the kid with ADHD who rushed through the whole thing just so he could say, "I'm done!" Before each day's work, I added a How-To page taken from the textbook. That way when I was working with the kids I'd have an example, there at the table, without having to go to the board (and thereby turn my back on the room). When I left each table, they could refer to the example. If I had an aide in the class, or the kid left for a behavior room, whatever adult was working with them had a refresher and a guide to how the concept was being taught in my classroom.

Once I had assembled this magnificent artifact of teaching practice, I had to copy it 15 to 18 times, staple it and three-hole punch it. It typically ran about 20 pages or so. I'd usually make at least 8 more than the number of students. That way if a kid said, "I lost it...don't have it...left it at home...left it in my locker..." I could just drop another one down and say, "No problem, just turn them both in at the end of the week and I'll staple them together." Like a loyalty card. For your education.

I started to feel a little bad for the kids. There really was no way to avoid the work. Even if I had to send a kid out to the behavior room, they would take the packet, and the behavior specialist would have an example of the work with directions on what the kids should do. Sometimes the kids decided it'd be easier to stay in class and just learn it with everyone else.

That was one week. In one class. Week 4, Chapter 2, Section 1. I usually got through about Chapter 10 in a year. My reading class prep was just as intensive. Over my tenure I typically taught at least three subjects: math, reading, and a science co-teach. I fully prepped for earth science with my co-teacher. For that class I also shot vocabulary video, built a website with animated activities and games, and helped plan out labs. For some of my co-teaching, I prepped less, and consulted more, suggesting changes or additions. Some years I might teach five different subjects, including an extra remedial math class. One year I co-taught both life science and earth science. That's a lot of copies.

And also why teachers in movies made me laugh, maybe a bit enviously. As the plot unfolds, they go through their dramatic lives, show up at school, walk into the room, hold up a book and say, "Today, Chapter 4." Shoot, I'd think to myself. I wonder if I could get away with that.

Prep was also a time—our free space in the day, though often after we made our copies, ate a sandwich, and ran around the halls with papers for people to sign there were possibly seven minutes left. But then, doors closed to the world outside, we hung out, made each other laugh, and took off our teacher masks.

My colleague Miss L. had the best laugh—completely infectious and delighted, so my buddy Mr. R. and I did our best to bring it out—comparing me to Magnum P.I., inventing imaginary students, proposing ridiculous activities for Early Release Day (celebrate Mao's birthday? Free tattoos?), renaming Hangman "Suspended Person" so it would be less offensive and we could use it as a vocabulary game, or getting our teammate Miss T. to swear in Turkish. It took on the air of a 12-step group at times—"Hi, I'm Chris, and I'm a teacher," "Hi, Chris"—and it helped us bleed off some of the pressure, until it was time for the bell to ring, time for us to step back into the flow.

DECEMBER

Food

Other than bells, books and electricity, the most important thing required to run a school (that isn't funding) is food. Not cafeteria food, but the food teachers and staff bring into the classroom's everyday life.

In the classroom, food can be a powerful motivation, tied to curricular activities and attached to scholastic goals. For example, kids meet a behavior goal for two weeks and get a pizza party, kids meet a completion goal for a semester and get game day the last week, and a pizza party. In the Building, we brought in food for birthdays, at holidays, and for dances.

There was food in the teacher's lounge, food at conferences, food in the office, food down every back hallway and office, when people had baked and cooked and brought in fruit from their trees in early fall.

There were potlucks after school, and there was food for professional development, from donuts and coffee to bowls of fruit, a nutritionally-enlightened afterthought advocated for, and only eaten by, the health and PE teachers.

In our school, before the activities of the year slowly covered them with artifacts, room walls were blank and uniform, the hallways clean and bland, so we had to find some way to bind ourselves, in the way people usually did. Since food is love, and the school ran on love (at least in my opinion) we were always finding excuses to bring it in.

Eat it, share it, give it, earn it. Food is the hidden currency in the life of a school, and was the one thing we could use that didn't have a metric attached to it.

Hmong rice salad, pizza, cake, barbeque ribs, mole, tortillas, pizza, cake, Norwegian hot dish, pizza, cake, ice cream. Pizza. Also, pizza.

My theory on why pizza was the default food has three elements. First, it provided variations on a theme-with a few different collections of toppings, you could cover many preferences. Second, it came fast, and was modular. A stack of boxes, a roll of paper towels, good to go. Third, as mentioned before but worth repeating, by its nature it is built to be shared—sliced, fractioned, divisible by pretty much any number, allowing for appetite size. An often overlooked partner in the progress of American education—the pizza vendors of the United States.

The food we cooked ourselves and brought in was how we connected with the world. Welcome the kids—food, welcome the parents—food, welcome the teachers—food, welcome visitors—food. Since the school was our house, food was the way we made it our home, and we did so with great abandon, like people do everywhere. In the building, love, as much as people, lived on food.

Bells

E very year, I got my bell schedule, printed it out on the big poster maker, and studied the patterns, which could puzzle a Mayan astronomer. The only other enterprises outside of schools that run on such odd times are airlines, trains and subways.

20xx-20xx Bell Schedule

Warning Bell: 7:30
Period 1: **7:33 – 8:25 (52)**
Period 2: **8:29 – 9:21 (52)**
Period 3: **9:25 – 10:17 (52)**
Period 4: **10:21 – 11:13 (52)**
Period 5: **11:17 – 12:38 (81)**

Lunch 1: **11:16 – 11:41 (25)**
Class Start and End 11:45 – 12:38 (53)

Lunch 2: **11:43 – 12:08 (25)**
Class Start and End 11:17 – 11:43 & 12:11 – 12:38 (53)

Lunch 3: **12:13 – 12:38 (25)**
Class Start and End 11:17 – 12:10 (53)

Homeroom: **12:41 – 1:01 (20)**
Period 6: **1:05 – 1:57 (52)**
Announcements **1:58-2:00**
Dismissal **2:00**

The first couple days, kids barely made it to class, and I didn't much blame them. Sometimes, when I was working in multiple classrooms, I barely made it myself.

These bizarre divisions of the day make every teacher capable of really excellent mental math. A kid might ask, "Hey Mr. A.? How many minutes until third lunch?" Lunchtime was the most complex of all. Depending on the year I taught, it was either the fourth of seven periods, or the fifth of six.

The challenge with the mid-day period was fitting in three lunches to feed everyone. So in a six-period day, this ended up being three altered periods. A kid who had First Lunch had a 25-minute lunch, then a 53-minute period. Someone with Second Lunch had a 26-minute half-period, followed by a 25-minute lunch, then a second 26 minute half-period (refocusing attention after the break in second lunch period was no easy task). Kids with Third Lunch had a 53-minute period, followed by a 25-minute lunch. So, from the depths of fourth period, 31 minutes in, to be exact, he was asking me to calculate the differential between remaining time in fourth, through passing time, through the first two lunches in fifth, to the start of third lunch. I was so used to it at the time, I did it without even pausing.

Even as I pointed at a kid's paper with a Sharpie to emphasize a math concept, or took away someone else's headphones or a cel phone (I put them all in the Return Box, a locked box kept on my desk. Headphones were returned at the end of each period. Cel phones I had a one strike policy. I could see them once in a year, but the second time they went to the office, no appeal. I told them, "Your phone is like a shark in the ocean. I know it's there, but I don't want to see it."), and watched the doorway for an aide to pick someone up for social work, I rattled out the answer. Using the bell schedule shown previously, it was an hour and 21 minutes. At the time I did it in my head. As I write this, I had to open up a calculator to work it out.

One year we had a schedule in which every Thursday was extended homeroom, so one that day all the other periods were different lengths, except the one right before lunch. Lunch was inviolable, since we had to feed the kids. It was a constant, probably a legal requirement, and it would also be insane not to feed 13-year-old boys and girls for a whole day.

During standardized testing time, the bell schedule got ridiculous. The day started with three hours of tests, then we'd have first period when fourth usually was, fifth was the same, then second and third where fifth and sixth usually were. Those days I'd write a huge schedule up on the white board, then stand by the board, pointing out to kids where they needed to go.

The elaborate attention paid by the district to how many minutes kids spent in instruction was laughable, because the actual number of minutes they were involved in instruction didn't have much to do with how long the class was. I heard a lot of people say how much better the long suburban periods were, with their block schedules, and their A/B days, but I always felt it wasn't how much time you had, but what you made of it. I tried to do as much with 47 minutes as I could (when we had seven periods) and 52 minutes (when we had six).

The real advantage of six periods for the district was that it let you run a school with less teachers, aka less money. The disadvantage for the kids was that they no longer had extra periods for electives, which were, for many of them, the only high point in an otherwise really boring day. But that's another essay, and it isn't about minutes.

Time in a classroom was almost Einsteinian in its elasticity. If things were going well, classes passed in seconds. If it was a dragged-out day, if I was emotionally compromised, as happened sometimes, or I was sick, or the kids were sick, or anything that could act as a drag on the flow, the 15 minutes I spent in small group for my reading class could seem like 15 to Life.

Sometimes, I'd drag the class like a giant sack of concrete

through the lesson. Often, they'd pick up a spark, and run, and I felt the time less keenly. But when you pay attention to every second in your environment, both because it's your job, and because the kids need you to, the hours can seem like a lifetime and blink of an eye both.

Adding minutes to the schedule was likely a good idea, but I don't really think I changed anyone's life with an extra seven minutes. One time I showed my schedule to a family member and they said that if the business world had to run with that kind of precision, the Fortune 500 would collapse. Late, for us, was not an option.

Living inside such a schedule led me to this belief: Those that can, do. Those that can tell time, teach.

Professional development

Teachers continuously retrain—like doctors, accountants, lawyers and other people who are stewards of other people's interests. Except politicians, of course.

In a school, as part of the master calendar, a few days are set aside each year for professional development (PD). Far away from the front line, in what we called 360 (district headquarters), academic coaches talked in measured voices about a kid at one school, or a new initiative and the kickoff meeting that went with it; or even In the Building, in the relative quiet of the principal's offices, teams decided what new techniques teachers need to know.

Very few teachers will be arrogant enough to say they have nothing left to learn, but the barrage of new techniques, each fundamental in nature, often overlapping, frequently contradictory, was unique in my working experience. The reason there is very little overt resistance to the new techniques, which can focus on classroom management, reading techniques, ways of fostering learning through questioning, fundamental reading instruction, and new common standards (just to name a few), is that often PD days fall after October, which means everyone is bone-tired already, and PD makes a welcome break from the tumult and hullaballoo of everyday school life.

By the way, the kids are typically stunned by the fact that we continue our studies. "You gotta go to school? But, you're teachers!" As though we already Knew All Things, and just popped up out of the floor to teach each day, collapsing like airbags back into our cases when the bell rang at the end of the day.

PD days, I rolled up, grabbed coffee and a bagel, was willing to sit quietly and listen happily to just about anything. The speakers were often Formers, which was how I thought of Former Superintendents, Former Principals, Former Teachers. They were here among us to outline their programs, which, when implemented, would provide the gains we needed on standardized test scores. The programs didn't start off with those goals, but over the years, as we moved through the stages of No Child Left Behind (not unlike Anger, Denial, Acceptance, etc.), our school's Safe Harbor started to feel some serious groundswell and high winds as we approached Year 3 on the list.

I was not one of the teachers who rejected everything the Formers said out of hand. Those teachers very rarely let their feelings be known, since adults are experts at faking attention and participation, and almost universally the people at my school were good-hearted and earnest, and tried to implement everything we were asked to.

There was just so much of it. I started to feel like a novice golfer. Keep your head down, eyes on the ball, ease up left foot, weight on back foot, but also don't shift the weight, actually shift it but not yet; all of that in your mind and at least some of it contradictory, to the point where you basically feel like you are going to fall over.

It got to the point where we were working within

practices mandated by federal legislation, which became state law, we had district mandates, some had Special Ed mandates, our principal also had her own building training and mandates, and then I had my own personal practices.

I ended up drawing a map of my classroom. That way I could keep track of which things I did where. For example, by a little square I drew to represent my screen up front I wrote; Accountable Talk, Universal Design For Learning, Read180 Best Practices; because while I was standing up there, I might use a technique from all, some, or just one of those bodies of knowledge and practice.

There were labels for the horseshoe-shaped table where I did small groups for reading, math and study skills; there were labels for the tables where the kids sat, and so on. By the time I was done, I counted 17 different sets of practice and technique, overlapping at least half the time and contradicting each other completely at least 10 percent of the time. All of these practices were mandated. I was trying to do the best I could, for the kids who walked in my door every day, but it wasn't easy. That's why some people just plain didn't do the new practices.

So I'd grab a bagel, sit down, and enjoy the incredible, leisurely passage of time uninterrupted by crisis, lack of concept comprehension, interpersonal student-driven stress, building-wide incident, or even the usual sounds of 800 kids in the building. After a few hours, though, I started to get jumpy. It was too quiet, too orderly. I wasn't used to it, and it caused a mild Teacher PTSD.

The PD we had at the district level was even more of a

visit to Other Worlds. I participated in something called Professional Learning Communities, a really good idea. Teachers who taught the same subject came together to share practices and thoughts that would improve teaching across district. I ended up in the Math PLC, since we already had someone at Reading, and I got the Science information from my co-teacher in Science.

A lot of the people in the Math PLC were Shoulds, a sub-type of teacher who spend a lot of time discussing what other teachers Should have done with the kids when they were in other grades. To me this was like complaining about injustice, which shouldn't happen; or the Vikings getting back to the Super Bowl, which should happen, but hasn't. Not that Science and English were immune to Shouldism, but I heard, "These kids should have learned ____ in ____ grade." Indeed, they should have. But they didn't, and they're in your class. So, what are you going to do?

They reminded me a little of tradesmen. I rebuilt my house once, and though I did a lot of the work myself, I also had a lot of tradesmen in. They had a tense unique to their world, which I called Trade Third Person Past. They'd look at a wall and go, "So, what was He doing here? Don't know why He did that." "He" was anyone who had ever worked on the same part of the house before, a shadowy, faceless incompetent who had always done the wrong thing. For Shoulds, in teaching "He" took the form of elementary teachers, of middle-school teachers, anyone down the instructional chain, depending on who was complaining.

But I wasn't. It was a day off, a field trip. Sometimes,

when I was able to go with people from my building, we even Went Out to Lunch, like actual adults, instead of jamming a sandwich in our faces during prep as we did 16 other things in 51 minutes. We were like honest to God real white-collar people. We felt like we were free, playing hooky, taking a mini-vacation, because all we had to do was listen.

We did learn, it kept the edge off, and like the holidays for the kids, maybe that's another reason why it happened.

Teaching: a transcript
December 13, 20xx. Period 3: 9:49 a.m.-9:56 a.m.

I am sitting in the front of my science co-teacher's classroom, on a stool, working on a concept map, which is displayed on a screen behind me using a document camera. My co-teacher, Mr. M., is working the back of the room, calling individuals to focus and adding in facts. We change places frequently during class. Prior to this exercise, I was the one in the back of the room.

ME: **"Gentlemen, eyes up front. Need your attention."** (Still some talking. I wait.) **"Need your attention."** (I wait. One kid still talking.) **"That's 30 seconds on dismissal."** (Some shifting of weight but no complaints. It was not that way at the beginning of the year—it took a couple of weeks of them earning two minutes or more, and much grumbling, to get the expectation set.) **"We work through this concept map well, you can maybe win that 30 seconds back. Subject today—types of volcanoes. Think back to Section 1 of this chapter."** (This statement is designed to Activate Prior Knowledge, enable the kids to connect their current knowledge to new information. The concept map includes three large blank ovals. My pen is poised above one.) **"Volunteer—what is the name of the first type of volcano we learned about?"** (Hand shoots up.)

DESHAWN: "Shield volcano."

ME: "Correct." (I write **Shield Volcano** in the first oval.) "**Characteristics? Volunteer?**" (DeShawn's hand comes up.) "**Thanks DeShawn—you already weighed in—stand by to help out though.**" (Hand comes up.) "**Jorge?**"

JORGE: "Tall, shield shape, fast-moving lava, and…"

ME: "**Good details—wait, hold up, gotta leave room for other people here.**" (As he speaks I draw smaller ovals connecting to the first large one.) "**Random Call. Mr. M., who's next?**" (My co-teacher has a clipboard with a list of kids' names, scrambled alphabetically, which we use to get responses and as an engagement strategy, calling randomly over time on everybody in the class. It usually takes a couple of days to get through the list.)

MR. M.: "**Murphy.**"

ME: "**Murphy. Remember, you can use the book or notes.**" (Study skill reminder—metacognitive: tell the kids what tools they can use to answer a question. Pause, watching Murphy. Catch movement in the back corner, kid's head on a lab table.) "**Charles. Eyes up front please.**" Pause. "**Charles.**" (I wait. He looks up.) "**Murphy, what do you have?**"

MURPHY: (guessing) "**Violent eruption?**"

ME: "**Can somebody tell me if that's correct? Quintin?**"

QUINTIN: "Nope, that ain't correct."

ME: "Good. Why?" (Higher order-thinking. Concept association. I write ? **Eruption** in the oval.)

QUINTIN: "Honestly? I have no idea." (Class laughter.)

ME: "Appreciate that. DeShawn, you were on deck to answer something. Any ideas on that one?"

DESHAWN: "The type of lava?"

ME: "Good start. Say more about that." (Silence.) "Who can add to that? What does lava type have to do with a shield volcano not having violent eruptions?" (Wait time—three seconds. Long enough to change rhythm, not too long to break the flow.) "Mr. M., random call please."

MR. M.: "Luis."

ME: "Luis, tell me this—What is the opposite of a violent eruption?" (Return to basic concept—compare and contrast strategy. DeShawn has hand up. Silence. Wait time.) "Meng, help him out."

MENG: "Quiet eruption."

ME: "Correct. Now, Luis, you're still up. What type of lava goes along with a quiet eruption? Remember when Mr. M. did the demonstration with the oatmeal, the honey, and the water up here on Monday?"(General agreement, connect to prior experience.) **"That was like the lava type in this case. And we said the oatmeal had something called...?"**

CHARLES: (From under the lab table, where he sits on the floor.) **"Viscosity."**

ME: **"Excellent answer. Charles, you are correct. Also, need you to have a seat, in your seat."** (I wait. He doesn't get back on his stool.) **"Charles, we need to move on, you're holding us up, looking at 30 seconds for the class if you don't get back in your seat."** (Kid at his table whispers to Charles. He gets back in his seat.) **"OK, good, no 30 seconds there."** (Mr. M. moves to the back of the room, stands near Charles, who turns to look at him. Mr. M. is looking forward at me, but right behind Charles. Doesn't look at Charles. Proximity.) **"So what kind of viscosity does a quiet eruption have? Luis and group answer please."** (That way Luis is still held accountable, but others can back him up in case he still doesn't know, so he won't be embarrassed and will answer in the future.)

GROUP ANSWER: (Luis and a couple kids call out) **"Low viscosity."**

ME: **"Correct."** (I write **Low Viscosity** next to **Quiet Eruption**.)

ME: **"So we got a set of connections here: quiet eruption, low viscosity, and also, this kind of lava builds up gradually, layer after layer to form—volunteer?"**

TYLER: "**Shield volcano.**" (I circle the words **Shield Volcano**).

ME: "**That's it. Good job, gentlemen. You've earned the 30 back.**" (I get up, still facing the room, and erase a 30 Mr. M. had written with dry erase marker up on the board behind me. The number serves as a visual cue, so the kids always know where the time penalty is at any given moment.)

ME: "**So here's the job: Write down the characteristics I did, then draw and label a picture of a shield volcano. You've got two minutes, work with your table.**" (The kids sit four at a lab table.) "**You can speak in a normal voice, position is in your seat. Charles, you are in your chair, writing.**" (Wait time. Eye contact, scan class. Wait time for start signal.) "**OK, you can begin.**" (Mr. M. comes up to the front of the classroom. We speak in our normal voices.)

ME: "Running long." (I look at the clock. We are 24 minutes in, 28 left, with three other activities to do.)

MR. M.: "Yeah."

ME: "Viscosity took a while, but I wanted to make the connection so they could do the other types."

MR. M.: "Makes sense. We can fill it out and use it as an APK (Activate Prior Knowledge) tomorrow morning." The kids talk and fill out the ovals.

ME: "What's up with Charles?"

MR. M.: "Nurse said he missed his meds his morning. He took them in second, should be ok later."

ME: "Right."

MR. M.: "Let's wait 30 seconds, then switch. I'll call 'em back, we can start vocab for Section 4."

ME: "Sounds good." I walk over to the document camera, turn the switch to off. Mr. M. goes to his laptop and cues up a video to display.

MR. M.: **"Gentlemen, stop what you are doing."** (He has a powerful teacher voice. I don't think he has to brace his stomach muscles like I do.) **"Eyes up front, need your attention."** (Waits). **"You are at zero seconds on dismissal right now."** (Reminder of behavior rules, status of penalties.) **"Switching gears—you will finish the concept map as we go through the chapter, we will come back to that tomorrow morning. Now—we are going to watch a video about the three types of volcano. Remember, you are looking for and listening for characteristics. Here we go."**

Here we go, he says. That's his cue. Sometimes I shot video of our vocabulary, to post on our website. Mr. M. said that every time we started an activity. I asked him about it, he said he didn't even know he did it.

This is seven minutes of a six-hour school day, 13

percent of one period, and I taught five in a day. Those were the streams of thought running through my head as I taught, and that is truly how hard we all had to think, and on that many levels, with that many variables.

That's why I sometimes I slept at dinner, my head on the table, as my kids cleared the dishes, and why I spent the first two weeks of summer break napping. Teaching is to mental effort what the Tour de France is to cycling. The longest marathon, a journey up a mental Everest. Since then, I've never had to do anything remotely as difficult.

Holidays

I always envied my sister- and mother-in-law. Both of them worked in a district in Chicago that got all the holidays. Not just Christmas, Thanksgiving, the usual, but Hanukkah, High Holy Days, Rosh Hashanah, and everything else. All they were missing were Family Day and Canada Day.

We had the usual holidays, but my suggestions that we make Ramadan a month off since we had so many Somali students fell on deaf ears, for some reason. Think of the money it would have saved for the cafeterias. Of course, all the kids who weren't Muslim might have been somewhat upset that they didn't get to eat.

Holidays manifested themselves In The Building as dances, activities, bunches of roses borne down the hallway by student government (Valentine's Day), but most of all, their main side effect was conversation.

It was often the parties that led to your first real dialogue with the kids you taught. My first year I was still a hard-ass, and wanted to insure lots of instruction time, so I'd still be working when all the other teachers had parties in their classes. The last couple days before Christmas typically became party and movie day. Before I knew about the Unspoken Master Calendar, I was the only one asking them to do anything, and by their sullen compliance, and sometimes outspoken rebellion–"How come you the only one having class?"–I quickly realized that this not going to work.

So as that first year went on, and in the years that followed, I went along with the rest of the teachers, thankfully. It was a chance to celebrate whatever holiday was coming, which means more when you have had less of them, like my students. It not only allowed us to take a break from the Learning Machine, but often, when everyone was occupied, kids were watching a movie or playing a game, it was the time I first got to know individual kids as people.

Many years this happened just before Christmas break. I wasn't holding their hands over the candle, establishing community, moving desks around, moving people from class to class to make the whole thing work. The pieces had fallen into place. They knew my routines. I had established I was an Acceptable Teacher (my room and the world I built was consistent enough to be understood and they could live in it day after day). They had gotten to know me, but I still didn't really know them. So during those parties and holiday fun days, we could talk at leisure without endangering the fragile balance between authority and fun.

Holidays always featured specially-themed meals in the cafeteria (Christmas pizza?). The student government sponsored gift collections, which I though was truly heroic because some of them were giving gifts full well knowing they weren't going to get many themselves.

We had Labor Day, which marked the start of the year, Halloween trick-or-treating, Secret Santa, MLK, Hmong New Year, Cinco de Mayo, and Memorial Day, which marked the end of the year. Through it all, on holidays we gave ourselves, at least for a few days here and there, permission to hang out with the kids with whom we spent so much time.

The strangest thing I ever did at school was connected to a holiday. My supervising teacher for the tenure process was a speech therapist, and a committed Harry Potter fanatic. During my first year she convinced me that all the teachers intended to dress as characters from the books, and that since I had dark hair (still, at that time) and round glasses, I should be Harry. To set the stage, I should be clear that dressing up for any reason, especially Halloween, is not my thing. For example, as I shepherded the kids around the neighborhood each year for trick or treating, I was invariably a lumberjack—flannel shirt and ax. Got the job done. But I imagined I had tenure on the line in this case, so I very grudgingly allowed my wife to get some sort of robe together, and to draw a lightning bolt on my head.

When I got to school Halloween morning, you guessed it, only a couple of other first-years had dressed up. As I scuttled at warp speed to my classroom I ran into a girl from my math class who had given me intense grief in my first couple months. She was as tough as they came, and when she saw me in the hallway, she just smiled. "Harry Potter." She moved her head in an extremely complex motion that implied both contempt and amusement at the same time. "Uh-huh." I tore my robe off on the way in the door to my room, and my forehead was rosy for two hours, I scrubbed my head so hard.

But mostly, the biggest holiday benefit, for both students

and teachers, was just Making It All Stop, even for a couple of hours. And that, the same reason for all holidays, kept us sane, and able to get back to it another day.

.

JANUARY

Lanyards

My second year, our principal bought everyone a lanyard, blue and gold (Panther Pride) with our last names woven into the tough nylon. There was a key ring that came with the lanyard, but within a couple days it became clear there was no way it would hold up to my keys, so I got a heavy duty one.

Some people didn't like having a lanyard, but I wore it gladly. For me it was talisman, toolbox, and/or millstone, depending on how I felt that day.

My first couple of years, I would "forget" to take it off after school and "accidentally" wear it into the coffee shop near home in the afternoon. I was proud of it—our equivalent of a cop's badge and gun. Saint Paul Public Schools, baby. Local 28, all the way.

Which was one of the pins some people put on the lanyard. Union pin, SPPS pin, all kinds of other stuff. I never went in too much for the pins and badges—made me feel too much like a TGIFridays waiter.

For me the main thing on the lanyard was my keys. The number of keys corresponds to time in rank for a teacher. My first year, I only had the key to my own room. After seven years, I had keys for my room, the science office, the science storage closet, hallway door keys for a couple of doors across from one of my rooms, where the EBD teacher would lock the door and the kids had to wait in the hallway, and several storage cabinet keys. The keys had a rhythmic, almost pleasant swinging weight, and when I walked fast down the hallway they jingled, which was in some cases like belling the cat. I'm sure there were multiple occasions where lockers were slammed just before I came around the corner, the young scholars hearing my jingling approach, hiding something.

The lanyard also became my toolbox. At any given time, I'd have at least three different kinds of pen hanging off my lanyard, and a mechanical pencil. There would be a colored sharpie (for drawing explanations on worksheets); a highlighter, for the same purpose; and one mechanical pencil for the kids early on in the period that said they didn't have a pencil. Since I dismissed class with the kids sitting down, it gave me a chance to get the pencil back, and never have to leave a kid unsupervised to get a pencil, or walk back to my desk and turn my back on the room.

On the other hand, taking off the lanyard, the jingling passing over my head at the end of a long day in March, walking to my car in 10 below weather, felt like taking off a backpack when you hike, a lifting of weight literally and figuratively. Or getting out from under that millstone, if it was a really bad day.

I was done, and the lanyard coiled between the driver's and passenger seats, to remain there until tomorrow, when I would once again sling it, jingling, to its place around my neck. A symbolic act—I was stepping into The Building, and into the flow.

310: IN THE BUILDING

The union

I had mixed feelings about our union. Full disclosure—I come from a labor background so strong that as a kid, my family drove an hour into Honolulu to picket supermarkets selling non-union grapes during the time of Cesar Chavez. My uncle, a university professor, organized these expeditions. My senior year in high school I wrote a long paper on The Jungle, Upton Sinclair's epic saga of the deprivation and suffering of Slavic meat packers in Chicago. Fight the power indeed.

So when I got my first union card from Local 28, AFT, Saint Paul Public Schools, I was thrilled to take my place in the long line of people who had fought for their rights. I was, and still am, a believer in the idea of unions.

My thoughts on our teaching union, though, changed over the years to something more complex. As I learned my way around the classroom, I didn't think much about the union. I thought it was very cool that they went off and asked for things for us, that they had our best interests in mind, and were there for us so we could keep teaching knowing that our livelihoods and long-term prospects were being looked after by peers, by people who understood. This was in the mid-2000s, before the gradual erosion of funding for public schools began, before No Child Left Behind took full effect, and at a time my state had a surplus. The system was not

117

under pressure of any kind. There was money, and all was well.

By the late 2000s, that had started to change. The state no longer had a surplus. The requirements of NCLB were becoming an increasingly burdensome unfunded mandate that affected the way teachers went about their business every day. It was about this time we started to face annual 20 million dollar deficits in the district budget. Staff size started to shrink. Teachers were offered retirement incentives. First year, non-tenured teachers were released. Talk began of school closures, and the arts, especially music, were cut.

The twin pincers of less staff and more pressure to make NCLB targets, along with an increasing amount of due process for our group of special ed teachers, began to close on us.

People started looking year to year. A future including fewer special ed teachers meant an automatic increase in caseload. I calculated once that the paperwork, scheduling, and other required work for a single IEP took approximately three hours for a kid you knew, and four for a kid you didn't yet know (a seventh-grader, for example). Doing a full reevaluation took between eight and 10 hours for test administration, writing, and other admin work. When I started, I had a caseload of 15. My last year, I had a caseload of 25.

This is relevant because the union's response, knowing well our challenges related to dwindling budgets and increasing workloads, led to two outcomes that disconnected me from the process.

First, they failed to really enable any kind of change in work requirements. What we needed was help reviewing our documentation to be sure we were in compliance. When I started, we had specialists who knew all the regulations and reviewed everything we wrote. Having reviewers meant we could turn in IEPs and ESRs (reevaluations) without worrying about them afterwards. They'd be done, and we could move on to the next document. Those positions were cut in my third year, we asked the union to find a way to get them back, and the union could not.

Once we lost the compliance people, we missed landmines in the regulations that would come back and bite us. During the busy season, January to April, when I'd have two to three meetings a week, if I discovered an addition or change, it meant I'd be up until 1 a.m. a couple of times that week fixing it.

Instead, the union focused increasingly on things that seemed less important to me. There was much talk of how we didn't have to sub for general ed teachers, that we should not do certain duties around the school. But those duties were one of the only things that connected us to all the kids and the school as a whole unit. Personally, I liked subbing in the other classrooms. I got to meet other kids, and other kids saw me more as part of the school staff, not just a guy down a back hallway. I also liked the extra chaperoning and other tasks that later were no longer asked of us.

The real disconnect came when the district started cutting positions wholesale. One year we went from 72 teachers to 62. We talked amongst ourselves of how we'd be willing to take a small pay cut, so people could keep their jobs, but also so the school wouldn't lose some richness and capability that were going away as the arts diminished, as the electives shrank and as the school lost some of its spark.

I mentioned that to a teacher who was very active in the union and she looked at me like I had three heads. She was adamant that we couldn't give, that the administration was negotiating in bad faith already and if we made an offer like that we'd just be showing critical levels of weakness. I understood what she was saying. At that time we had a superintendent who had come in from DC riding on a wave of metrics and anti-union sentiment. She made several impressive PowerPoints, then departed for a larger school district three years later.

The super was, by the way, a poor choice from the start, since she had only been a classroom teacher for a year, and that year had been as a photo teacher. The rest of her career had been in admin, so she had a serious credibility problem in the rank and file.

I hadn't forgotten my union roots. I just thought we would all benefit from some flexibility, that we could help keep people employed, maybe ride this thing out. Not a position our union took. In my side conversations with peers, when we had time for that, which was basically never, others took the same point of view. A second group seemed indifferent, like, well, they always took care of us before, and we're stuck with them, so there you go.

I do know the one time I thought about going to the union, in a situation for which it is specifically designed, I hesitated. I wasn't sure they could keep the situation confidential. It didn't involve kids, or I wouldn't have waited a second. It involved myself (a non-tenured teacher), a friend of mine (a newly-tenured teacher), and a teacher with 30 years in the district. Myself and my colleague believed the other teacher was out of line in some of his dealings with us. But we didn't trust the system, and said nothing. He was later fired after all, for harassing a kid so egregiously that he had to be let go. Though our problem with him was different than the cause that forced his release, I wish I had said something. But I'm as sure now, as I was then, that I would not have been protected.

When I see vilification of teachers' unions and their intransigence, from people who have no idea what goes on in a classroom, I still defend the unions. Everyone thinks they can teach and everyone thinks they know what makes a good education. I'll admit unions are doing some things they shouldn't; but by and large they still serve a useful purpose. They should, however, be careful that they don't fossilize, or they will disappear. Then the protections they provide will be gone, and teachers will be used up and disposed of like other white-collar people are now, except for a third of the salary.

The unions may not be rearranging the deck chairs on the Titanic, but they are definitely pumping water out of the wrong places in the ship.

Visitors

As we rolled through our tightly defined days as teachers, ruling the tiny kingdoms of our classrooms, we always intermixed with a steady stream of visitors to the school. They looked in through the doors, observing the flow and chaos; patterns made of voices and hands on shoulders and the occasional name barked across the commons. They peered out through the glass in the office, seated, waiting to talk to an administrator: parents, district people, coaches, testers, reporters. They were in the school, but not of it.

The metaphor that always sprang to mind was free divers, drifting above the reef of the building, floating, as just below them schools of fish scurried, predators chased, eels hid in their rocky dens. As a reef denizen, I was often called up to rise up into the mid-water column, to say hello, point out a teaching practice, or just keep doing what I was doing, as they watched me. Performance anxiety, writ large: keep your eyes on the ball, and watch out for X, no meds today so we don't want him to put on a show for the district people.

I mentioned the Metric-PowerPoint superintendent and her credibility crisis earlier, the way it sprang from our disdain that she had taught for only a year, and the moment she could aspire to the adminisphere she fled, away from the paper bits, the electronic grinding echo of the bells, and the smell of Axe. Yeah, good for you. At one year in you don't even have the beginnings of long-term sleep deprivation or mild PTSD.

When she did visit, she swept down the halls like a general visiting front-line troops, looking for evidence of her five-point plan in action. Mostly all saw were sweaty, slightly confused preteens trying to navigate the shoal waters of early puberty, and a bunch of teachers doing their best to get them over the rocks.

Our school also periodically served as a polling place, and at those times the commons became even more of an aquarium. Kids flowed around the center area near the stairwells, where booths had been set up. An AP stood in the space to keep things calm. The voters would stroll in through the front doors, watching the kids go by like they were at Sea World, the kids peeling back and around the banisters as they went about their business.

Which mostly involved yelling and having crushes and being mad at people and forgetting their homework and thinking about the game they had that night and if maybe they'd finally beat Murray this year.

I was one of the teachers that served occasionally as a stop on the tours. Once my science co-teacher and I had visitors from a wealthy family intending to give a large grant to the district foundation, and interested in the way we were co-teaching. So in our classroom, we had six adults, clustered around an unused lab table in the back of the room, awkwardly perched on middle-school sized stools, trying to look like they weren't there, with maybe 20 or so eighth graders also trying to pretend they weren't there.

No pressure, by the way, but the donation could be big. We had our days all planned out always, so it was only a matter of running the machine as usual, and it went well. But it's a degree of scrutiny not a lot of professions have: Athletes, maybe doctors in an operating room with med students, people in public life. But middle-level power plant managers, chefs, insurance agents, they normally don't have people looking at them like they are in a zoo. Watching —watching and judging.

If the visitors came before November, I could be nervous. After that point I was just exhausted, so I hardly noticed them, until about March, after which I was so happy that we were getting on towards the summer that nothing bothered me.

I always wondered what they thought about it all, what it all looked like to them that I couldn't perceive, with my jingling lanyard of keys, caffeine-driven survival-fueled adrenaline rush and dry erase marker-stained fingers. I was never going to know. They were of the Outside, I was of The Building. Quite literally worlds apart.

Socialized

Anyone seeking the unsung heroes of the American public school system need look no further than a social worker's office. At my school, there was a rule in effect far more draconian than any 80-20 rule. The fact was, there were 10 needy kids who had the same effect on classrooms and the school's daily operations as tactical nukes. Call it the 1-80 rule.

When these kids arrived in a classroom, they Arrived. They might make it in the door, but they were not able to run with the program for long. So then they Left. Always with plenty of drama. For some of these guys, it was not the typical acting up. It was shut-down-whole-classroom kind of behavior, major problems in the halls, or catastrophes in the lunchroom.

I don't criticize them for it. Though many kids struggled with the effects of poverty, violence, homelessness, mental illness and just plain emotion, there were a handful of kids for whom these problems were epic and insurmountable, for whom the school, its structure, its rhythm and its requirements were simply not navigable.

Those were the kids you'd find interacting with the social workers. Somehow, this group of essentially saint-like human beings—and I don't use the word saint lightly—were able to coax, cajole, reassure, threaten, incite, invite, invoke and inveigle these kids into the classroom—most of the time.

Sure, sometimes the kids had to leave class, were processing something terrible, or were just overtaken by yet another episode in the almost unreal saga of their lives, but always Miss M., in our case, was there for them.

The attitude of teachers to this service was varied. I'm not exactly sure how real it was to them—there were some who clearly felt that it was babysitting and coddling, but I don't think they had a lot of experience with those particular kids. The idea that kids could have essentially overpowering struggles that would keep them out of the classroom much of the time just didn't compute with them.

I knew it was real because I had a kid who was one of the frequent fliers. We tried discipline, rewards, changed his schedule many times, time with all kinds of people, but for whatever reason, he was one of the kids running in the hall, the kids for whom the whole thing might not work.

Because he missed so much school, and in fact did have a learning disability, which was basically obscured by his behavior, the longer the school year went on, the harder it got for him, so by May he had missed another year.

But somehow, Miss M. never gave up on him. She worked with home when she could get them there, she worked with the school, she worked with me, she worked with everyone. She was on their side but she was also on the school's side, and I honestly don't know how she managed that day after day, week after week, year after year.

The kind of support she could give was all they could take. Some kids actually were able to get a handle on their trouble enough to make it through, in a way, and I have often wondered whether if at some point it all kicked in and they were ok.

She would take them all in her room, drifters and time bombs and the quiet, quiet ones who never said a word. There was a student once who was a selective mute. Something had happened to him, and he never spoke at school again after second grade. But somehow, over the course of his eighth grade year, Miss M. got him to say a word. A minor miracle, in fact, because speech is trust, and communication is all.

I have no doubt where Miss M. will go when she passes out of this mortal plane. If there isn't a heaven, they need to make one for social workers.

Disabled list

There's a certain point in any sports season when injuries start to crop up on a team. Wear and tear, sudden injury or unexpected off-field accidents lead to people being on the bench. Teaching is no different. One of my early mentors told me, "You want to call in sick, you better be holding one arm in the other hand, because otherwise you really, really have be In The Building."

Because we get the whole summer off, teachers are the least likely people amongst any group I've ever worked with to call in sick. Part of the reason for that is purely selfish. If you teach five periods a day, often three different subjects, you can't just suddenly not come in. Even if you have your week planned out, the kids may not yet have the materials ready for a day you're not there, or it's the kind of activity you can't really have a sub do, like a lab, or a key concept you need to cover for a test.

To call in sick, sometimes you have to go in the day you are actually sick, and gut it out through seven hours, so that you can prepare to be gone the next day. This was very common. You'd see people hanging by a thread, especially if it was a Monday, so they could get something prepped up for the next day.

I saw people lying on the floor on their prep periods dizzy but trying to make it until 2 p.m., people throwing up in bathrooms, people leaning against white boards. My science co-teacher, a big guy (6'1", about 240), sometimes had back troubles related to his time playing football and hockey. I'd come into the classroom, not having seen him that day, and he'd be on a stool, in front of the classroom, motionless. He couldn't even move his head. He'd control his class by voice alone, and have kids come up and do things. Many times this happened both Thursday and Friday; but he'd rest over the weekend and be back Monday.

I have a number of herniated disks, so I was no stranger to that sort of situation. Occasionally, I'd get back spasms, some so strong that if they hit me when I was standing up, I'd actually fall over. I wasn't going to miss a day, because I could still think and talk, so I brought in what I called my Teaching Stick, which was basically a cane. I'd use it when I had to do stand-up lectures, which for me wasn't a lot of the time, so that when the spasms hit, I could just clutch the stick, and thus not fall over. They would hit me in mid-sentence, I would pause, then roll on.

Another thing that came to get me over the years was plantar fasciitis, from standing up too long. Which, if you are a teacher, goes with the territory, and, what was my alternative? I had to move around the room, standing still was not an option, so I went through the better part of three years walking around on some pain related to that. Up to that point, the injuries made sense: I had the herniated disks from surfing and other sports, and plantar fasciitis made sense as well, from standing.

But what happened in my last year was a little weirder,

and kind of chilling. I had an incredibly low energy level and felt so off that I went to a doctor who eventually figured out I had non-specific swelling in many of my internal organs. I was like, what the hell does that mean? But I took some oral cortisone and went back into The Building. It turned out to be stress-related. That was the year I wrote IEPs five nights a week, because my caseload had increased so much.

The kids actually expected this kind of hardiness from their teachers. In working-class culture, you just work, you don't call in sick, because if you call in sick you don't get paid. They didn't admire this kind of approach, I think they just expected it, since it was what all the adults in their lives did.

Choosing a sub was important. A good sub could carry the class forward at least a small distance while you were gone. When I first started out, I'd plan activities for the subs to do, wanting to treat them fairly and with respect as teachers. They did do what they could, but when you got a random sub, the chances of that were much less likely. I ended up having two subs I used all the time. One was Mr. F., a part-time musician and general appreciator of life. Sub teaching was the way he made it through the world, but he was interested in his music and his outside activities, which I never quite figured out, but he was always "Busy, busy man, you know how it is."

The kids generally liked him, and when I could get him I would. Another was Miss P., who had been a teacher at the school, retired, and now was basically the designated sub for all of the special ed teachers. She was very reliable, I could ask her to do some good work with the kids, and they all knew her since she was In the Building all the time, working for various teachers. In fact she was probably there more than some notable exceptions amongst the teachers.

Having said that teachers were incredible hardasses who worked through agony, I must also admit that when there were exceptions, they were quite spectacular. One was an aide who worked in another program, who went through so many excuses— including fires in his mobile home, legal troubles, and more individual diseases than a lab rat at the CDC—that at one point the principal actually drove out to his house to see if he was even there, which he wasn't. He tried to put a brave face on it, but after that he was done. When she arrived at his trailer and there was no sign of a fire, which had ostensibly happened the week before, only his union status kept him from being fired.

Another teacher I knew in my first couple years was gone almost constantly. She taught the developmentally-delayed kids, and when she was gone, her aides had to scramble to cover for her. At first, other teachers covered for her too, but after a while people were like, Really? Again? That was another reason people didn't call in sick with no notice, because the minute you did, someone else was carrying your load for you. If it happened once in a while, no big deal, but happening constantly became a problem for the whole staff. The more that happened, the more unruly the kids got; they may or may not like their teachers, but the one thing they disliked most of all was change. They want their world and the people they see every day to be the same, so being gone a lot made a teacher's life difficult when they got back.

Mental health days were also common. You'd hear people say quietly, on a Tuesday, "I feel like I might be getting sick on Thursday." They'd prepare everything so they could be gone, never on a Monday or Friday, but in between, because some days you just needed it to stop.

I did it myself at times. I'd somehow just coincidentally leave all the worksheets needed for the next day on my desk; get a sub the night before, so I could be sure someone was showing up for me, and then be able to tell the secretary the sub could use the materials I left on my desk.

Sometimes even mental health days weren't enough. There was one teacher who had what was basically a nervous breakdown. She was teaching life science, all 7th grade boys, and going into the year I was already worried for her. The teacher before her had been very solid— a tall, ex-volleyball player from Central Minnesota somewhere, kind, but tough as frozen earth. She had no trouble with the boys. She left The Building after five years, to become an office manager at her new husband's chiropractic practice.

The minute I met her replacement, I worried she was going to be torn to ribbons by the boys, and sadly enough, she was. In early October, she called in sick one day, then two, then three, then basically just said she wasn't coming back. Ever. Which led to a fair amount of scrambling, but a new teacher was found within a week, and ended up staying for years.

At certain times during the year, the white board in the office would be filled with a long list of teacher's names, all the people that were out. If there were a lot of teachers out, typically because of travel or training, or sometimes just because the disabled list had grown to that point, it was tough for everyone who was still there—that much change, especially in core classes, meant disruption and unease across The Building all through the day.

Officially, I got 14 days of annual sick time, but I don't think I ever used more than seven. When I left, I had accumulated more than 40 sick days, and I was only with the district for seven years. We all paid a price for it, but then again, we also got the summer off-season to recover.

For some teachers, even the off-season wasn't long enough. We had a great choir and music teacher, a man who was a major mentor figure for the African-American kids, whose back got so bad he had to take a year off. When he came back they assigned him to an elementary school, but eventually he could no longer do bus duty, or even stand up at all, and he was released by the district. It really is a job that can chew you up and spit you out, from a physical standpoint.

SPRING SEMESTER

.

FEBRUARY

Observations, tenure, and fear

When I started teaching in 2005, tenure was still A Thing, as the kids say. There were no serious storm clouds on the horizon of public education quite yet, though there were rumblings, and sudden odd shifts of wind. I didn't become a teacher for security's sake alone, but I did think there was a greater relative degree of safety in teaching–once you had earned tenure–than there would be in the fire-at-will, reorg-heavy, job-cutting jungle of corporate life.

For me, as a career-changer in my early 40s, a successful leap to tenure was life and death. I had decided to Do Some Good. That being said, with a wife and two kids, I really, really had to make it to a full-time permanent position.

In my district earning tenure was a three-year process. The first year, the union provided training, prompted by statistics clearly indicating that unsupported first-years left the profession like college kids streaming out of a bar at closing time. The minefield of discovering your practice, the emotional rollercoaster ride, the pain and joy that make up the life of a first-year teacher are well-documented elsewhere. I knew I had a lot to learn, and my district knew it too, so I had a lot of support. As a special ed teacher in my first year, I had monthly PD on how to fill out paperwork. My teaching practices were evaluated by my own mentor, a long-tenured speech therapist, and also by the district coaches. I knew they were there to help me.

At the very back of my brain, though, my reptile mind screamed in fear every time they walked into the classroom. What would they see? What would the kids do? They were watching, watching, and writing down little notes, and I saw, though apparently I didn't show it, the ruins of my career in every missed question.

During my first tenure observation, one kid who had never before given me any trouble suddenly stood up, yelled at me, and stormed out of the room. She was a very bright girl, one of the few examples of a true Arithmetic Learning Disability I ever met. She could read well, write well and was very articulate. But the operations of addition, subtraction and multiplication for her might as well have been a snake fight on Mars for all she could comprehend them.

She only went as far as the hallway, and with one foot in the door, so I could still watch the other kids, I talked her down off the ledge. My mentor wrote some notes, discreetly. As I reasoned with the girl in the hall, barking at the kids inside to continue the worksheet, in a tiny corner of my mind I was gibbering wildly, trying to formulate the words to explain to my wife that they in fact had decided I would not ever be a teacher, clearly had no business being in the classroom, and that hiring me had been a bad mistake, thank you very much.

I realized I was being hard on myself. Afterwards, under as much control as I could manage, I asked how I thought it had gone, anticipating the response—get the box and put your things in it. She just shrugged. "Nice job. Good lesson, and I like how you handled things with A. She can be a little irrational."

I actually did get released at the end of my first year. School ended, I went to an invigorating four-day post-school training for first-years sponsored by the union, and I was fired up for the next year. Then I got a message on my voicemail from the Area Assistant Superintendent.

I thought to myself, maybe I won an award (?) not really believing it, and that was not the case at all. She said there was no issue with my performance; in fact, she said I was recognized as a solid first-year. But I was non-tenured, so that meant I was also first to go.

The next call I got was from my principal, a close to 40-year veteran who played the school district like a violin concertmaster. He told me if I was willing to wait to take another job, he'd do his utmost to find a way for me to get back to my school. No promises, of course, but he was pretty confident that if things played out as they might, with retirements, and people getting married and moving away and the like, he'd find a place for me.

I hung up the phone and sat in stunned silence. What

the hell. After all that. But then I rallied. He had said he'd try to get me back. Through most of the summer, I worried. I didn't take another job, didn't even really start looking around until about mid-July. Instead of enjoying my summer, I had a knot in my stomach, as I played with the kids, barbequed, went windsurfing, all the things that should have been restorative after a brutal first year.

I thought a couple of times about the year to come, but then my mind backed, skipped away—why bother? There was a grey cloud in my future. That summer we embarked on one of the best family trips we ever took—we flew into San Francisco with a load of camping gear, and drove up the west coast with no fixed destination. Northern California, the redwoods, crossing the San Andreas fault, which in my weakened mental state I made into a metaphor for my career—as California goes, so go I, right into the sea.

Onward, up the coast to Central Oregon, to a place called Waldport. We had been driving for 14 hours, no place to sleep, kids tired in the back, until we saw a Vacancy sign left on along a long row of beach houses and low-slung motels.

It turned out there actually was no vacancy, but they took pity on us and stuck us in part of a mansion that had been rented out, but canceled at the last minute. In the morning, we saw grey whales offshore. That afternoon, I got a call on one quavering bar of reception from my principal, whom I could barely hear. Did I want to come back?, he asked. Are you kidding me? Yes!

So I was saved, not by chance, but by the consummate

bureaucratic skill of a veteran principal, by the spirits of the great grey whales offshore, by something. I never came that close again to getting cut.

The thing was, as the years went on, what I at first thought was a ridiculous fear, since even in my heart I never truly believed it would happen to me, actually did happen to a couple of people. I saw non-tenured teachers disappear in mid-year.

One teacher, call him Z., who I knew was struggling, vanished a week before the end of second trimester. I got an email from the principal, went down to see her, and she asked me, to cover his math class sixth period. I said sure. Tomorrow? Was he sick or something? She said no, he's not coming back. Could I cover for the rest of the year, she meant. This happened on a Friday, a week before the end of March, basically. I never did find out what precipitated it, but hopefully it was justified.

My second year, the observations continued. The paradigm had changed, I was not observed monthly, and in fact, I was only scheduled for two observations. By this time I was teaching outside the building, in one of the portables. I loved being out there. My favorite observation story comes from the two-period reading class in the little huts behind the school.

I was starting to get my systems in place, the classroom had some flow, but I was far from proficient. School-wide, we were using a new way of questioning called Accountable Talk—research-based, of course. (You could claim it was helpful to the kids if you gnawed publicly on their folders, as long as it was Research-Based). The method required using key phrases, which when internalized, would help them structure their thought and their language.

We put up little speech bubbles, displaying the phrases, all over the classroom, (District coaches looked for the bubbles during observation visits, listing them as Artifacts.) This one kid, very bright and very, very ADHD, was in small group when the principal came in to do an observation. I was relatively confident everything would go smoothly, since the class was well-trained and it was mid-year, but there was still that out-of-body experience of trying to teach and knowing that at the same time The Boss was watching you and writing down everything you did on a rubric.

As I worked though the lesson, the kid, who we will call A., (and with whom I had a full two-year debate regarding the truth about global warming) looked me right in the eye and started to string the phrases together. "Mr. A, (1) I'd like to say more about that, and (2) to add to what D. said. In the book, on page 16 (3), I observed this detail, about the dog and the taxi. Can you add to that for me (4)?" Then he smiled at me, knowing the principal could not see him. He knew exactly what he was doing. It was all I could do not to fall out of my little chair laughing.

The rubrics contained items like Cultural Sensitivity and Differentiation, Teaching Practice, and Classroom Environment. I could be rated on a scale of 1-3. I gave myself 1s and 2s in everything, when the review happened. We discussed them after the observation.

Sometimes it wasn't the principal, but the AP, and a

couple of times it was peers, working on their principal's license. That could be pretty awkward, although they'd typically be more lenient.

The fear dogged me out of the end of second year and into third. The third year, the paradigm for observation changed. There was a new system called Learning Walks, where we all watched each other teaching, big packs of teachers roaming around visiting classrooms. You could be teaching and have 12 teachers walk in, sometimes a one-to-one ratio, depending on the class. Everyone tried to be non-disruptive, but at that density, it was pretty much impossible; The kids were like—what the heck is going on here?

I still had observations, but I was getting comfortable in how I operated. First semester of my third year, I had an observation from my new principal. She sat in the back of my algebra class, brow furrowed, making notes. Eyes intent. I'm doing everything by the book, and some things I made up. I had unilaterally introduced standards-based grading in my class. No A's or B's, just concept mastery, or not. I then converted the mastery back into letter grades as appropriate.

The kids left, and I sat down with her (it was my prep) and I launched into a rapid-fire explanation of my system, pleading, I thought, once again, for my livelihood. I asked, finally, the question I had been dying to ask for two-and-a-half years. Did she think I'd get tenure? She answered, puzzled. Of course, she said. She was more concerned with how she could adopt what I was doing in my classroom to other places. I admit to a brief swift spell of near dizziness. Then I was good. It looked like, barring some major calamity,

I was going to make it.

Later, after I was a grizzled vet, I was paired with a first-year teacher. He was young, confident, one of an extensive family of St. Paul teachers, a near-dynasty. He was, it turned out, overconfident. I'd suggest some things, based on what I saw in his class, and he was like "No, I got this." I backed off, watched. He didn't have it at all. By the end of his first semester, he had people in his classroom every day.

They all said he appeared totally cool and collected. He said he had it all under control, didn't need any help. He was the opposite of my terrified non-tenure state of mind. At the end of the first year, he was cut. I remember being in the library, one of those terrible April meetings when they tell you who won't be coming back. Through some miscommunication, he hadn't been told. His face went blank. He never saw it coming.

I hated those meetings. My fifth year, they were cutting into the third years. I just barely made it. I had a mental image of running rapids. Scraping by, into a world at least of relative security. But that was the year they started combining schools, and that's another story.

Fights

People who are not involved in public education make a big deal out of fights at school. "Did you hear there was a huge fight at South, between Somalis and African-Americans?" they say at dinners or barbeques. "I don't know what's going on over there. The schools are just going downhill."

Like so many other things, when viewed from the outside looking in, a fight can look like a pretty big deal. Kids jumping over tables, food flying all over the place, lots of yelling. But like so many other things in a school, the fight itself is also just the tip of a very large iceberg.

It would be ridiculous, for example, to think that somehow the fight caught the administrators by surprise. Whatever the root causes of a fight are, not just the cataclysmic, school-sized fight, but every fight that happens in a school; they go back some distance in time from the actual event. By the way, to think that only inner-city public school kids fight is pretty oblivious. When kids from the middle- and upper-class fight, they don't usually do it at school. But it still happens.

In the school where I worked, fights fell into several main categories.

First, establishment fights. Typically happening in the first couple weeks of school, they marked alpha males from different elementary schools establishing their territory entering seventh grade, or eighth-grade transfers trying to make a name for themselves in a way that earned respect amongst the kids and scrutiny from the administrators and teachers. Those fights, by their nature, needed to be public, so everyone could see the new kid was a badass, and also were primarily for show, since the kids knew that by having the fight in the middle of the largest common area at passing time, it was guaranteed to be broken up quickly, and not too much damage was typically done. It also showed the school that the new guys "didn't give a ___" what happened to them, also part of establishing cred.

The second major time establishment fights occurred was right after semester break, when kids were being administratively transferred from one school to another, the last step before getting kicked out of the public schools altogether. Admin transfers were almost always a result of someone stepping in to give a kid a second chance, and most often the kids would show up in early February, right after first semester ended.

The last kind of establishment fight was the rarest, typically in April sometime, when a kid who had just moved up from Chicago, in from the suburbs, or just drifted in on the currents of homelessness, would show up at the school. We took everyone, always, so the kids were woven into the school fabric best as we could, but it was tricky at such a late date, and they often found ways to get attention in a pretty negative way. Very rarely, these happened between girls. But I will get to that later.

Another major category of fights I categorized as

145

Climate-Driven Conflict. The abyss, absolute zero of the Minnesota school year, begins in the second week of February, and lasts till the first week of March. It's not the holidays anymore, the weeks drag, it's a long time until spring break, and everyone—admin, teachers, staff and students—are hanging by a thread. The cold wears away at your soul and body, you stamp in shaking the latest 12-inch snowstorm from your boots, there are fewer staff and teachers in the halls since everyone is scrambling to keep up with their prep, and then, some annoying kid says something (just playing, dude) and a kid with a short temper snaps. These are non-premeditated fights, involving kids who surprise admins and teachers. You'd hear about it in second period—"Who got suspended? Really? Him?" Maybe things were rough at home, maybe there were money stresses, and sometimes a kid you thought wouldn't hurt a fly would just go off.

The category most incidents fell into was Someone is Saying Something About You fights. In the kid world culture of the urban working class (and no, that's not code for African-American, I'm talking about all the kids–white, African-American, Hmong, Latino and Native), this was not a minor matter. A kid's reputation is part of the armor that protects him (still not talking about the girls, but I will eventually) in the hallway.

So if a kid who was known as a fighter started talking trash about a kid who never did anything, the non-fighter kid still had to start talking to defend their honor. What prevented most of these fights from happening—and I would guess percentage-wise this type of fight was in the high 80s

146

percentile of total—was that middle-schoolers are biologically cocooned in a degree of self-absorption only retained into adulthood by pro athletes and investment bankers. Their world literally ends within 12 inches of their body. So when they talked, they often did it within earshot of teachers or staff, who could then activate the teacher intelligence network. In another odd disconnect, the kids never realized that all the teachers actually knew each other. I think they thought we sprang up from the floor when the bell rang, the way oxygen masks drop of out the overhead compartment on a stricken airliner. I even had several kids over the years who were stunned to learn I did not live in my classroom. "You mean, you go home?," they'd say.

For example, in first-period homeroom, taught by another teacher in my classroom, as I am doing my prep at my desk in the back of the room I hear Kid A talking trash about Kid B. I know both kids have algebra third period together; I get on the phone to the office during passing time. Speaking in School Hours Teacherese, a sparse and efficient code used by adults to communicate in short bursts during four minutes of passing time, I'd explain the situation, and ask for one of the school admins to have an AP call back. The phone would ring 10 seconds later. I tried never to call in anything I could handle, so they knew if I did call something in, it was significant.

I'd answer, still standing in the doorway, so I could see kids entering my room and also scan the hallway.

"Alper-Leroux."

"It's C. What's up?" the senior AP asks.

"Might wanna pull Kid A. from his second period. He's talking trash about Kid B. They had a history last year. They've got math together third period."

"Got it. Hey, is Kid A on an IEP yet?" C. is asking about the progress of due process for Kid A, who has a history of behavior problems, but none so severe that he is already on an IEP. He is being assessed now, but has not yet qualified, so his behavior has to be handled differently. Usually the APs are aware of the progress of the evaluations, but with so much going on, they don't always know.

"Nope. Meeting's next week I think. Kid A's still working with Mr. B. (A behavior specialist.)

"I'll talk to him."

"See ya." Hang up.

So C. pulls Kid A and Kid B separately from their second-period class. He sits them down individually, then together, to try to mediate before the fight happens. Maybe eight times out of 10, this works. If it's later in the year, it may not. Sometimes Kid A just is spinning, working up, until something has to happen. If the kid has been in several altercations, late in the year he might get a three-day suspension just to pull him out long enough for him to calm down.

Even if the kids say they are going to be ok, through the rest of the day everyone is watching them, listening to them, and listening to their friends. Lunch is important—if there are students running all over the place still saying Kid A is going to fight Kid B, Kid A might get pulled to sit in the principal's office through the first few minutes of dismissal, then run out to the bus at the last minute so nothing can happen. If, once the final bell has rung, the kids find each other out in the world, somewhere on a street corner, there's nothing we can do. We only have them seven hours a day, trying to keep the lid on long enough to get knowledge in. The rest is up to them, their families, their friends and whatever forces shape them. Our job is just to keep them from fighting long enough to make it through a day.

The last category, most severe and dangerous of all, was Girl Fights. At school, guys typically fought for show. Girls fought to do serious damage. When a fight starts you can usually interpose yourself between the two kids, they sense the presence of large adult bodies, and they pull their punches. You can corral them, and get in their way long enough to allow several people to surround them, never really holding or restraining them, letting them yell, and they will calm down. But not the girls.

One early September I was walking through the commons area during passing time when I saw one girl take off after another. A math teacher coming down the opposite hallway grasped what was happening, and took off after the girls as well. I was able to stand in front of one of the girls, the math teacher in front of the other. The fighting girls were punching between the two adults at each other, yelling and screaming, a high pitched keening I had until that point associated only with Irish funerals and whales. I literally had to keep moving and took a couple of body punches from the girl. She was strong. I found myself hoping she represented our school in some sport. Maybe MMA. She was so crazed she didn't even see me. If we hadn't been there at that exact second, I can't even imagine what would have happened before we showed up.

You know a fight is over is when the kids stop yelling, and either go silent or begin to cry. That took about three minutes with the girls, but with a 13-year-old girl that can seem like an eternity, especially if she is screaming in your ear. The girls also held grudges for years, whereas I saw boys who exchanged blows in September become buddies by December.

Luckily, there were hardly any girl fights.

In the end, I preferred that the kids were oblivious enough to play out their grand dramas where we could see them, deconstruct them, help them pass water under them, so they would smooth out. A high school teacher's experiences with fights would be very different from mine, but that's what I saw in our middle school world.

Coaches

For about a year and a half, I was a district coach. I left the classroom and chose to work on an initiative spanning several schools, helping teachers use technology in their classrooms to differentiate instruction. I did it for two reasons—at the time, I quite frankly thought I was about to crack, and it also sounded really interesting.

When I started teaching I eased into the job, handling what I later realized was a pretty low number of cases, and teaching classes that were less demanding. As I found my feet, I was drawn to harder classes, bigger cases, more complicated testing, and tried to push the boundaries of this new profession I had chosen.

There were also increasingly dense layers of regulations and paperwork sifting down on top of us—like snow, made of law. For each family that hired legal representation and forced through a small change in case regulations, every one of us had one more form, one more law, one more checkbox or test.

Over time, I had so many cases, so much going on at school, and so much going on at home, that I for the first time looked around for something else to do. The position I found was called UDL Coach. I looked into it, discovering that UDL stood for Universal Design for Learning, a philosophy that there were no average students, that all kids could learn given the proper way to do it, and that technology could be an avenue to make that happen.

This was preaching to the choir for me. We were already well into the school year, but I started to interview, even knowing I was going to put my school in a tough spot, to replace a teacher in mid-year.

It sounded fascinating, and that has always led me to trouble, toil and satisfaction over the years. I interviewed, showing the committee the website I had built for co-teaching, and talking about my belief system. The only thing I requested was that I could stay in my science co-teach period, both because I loved being in there, and for legitimacy. I had met coaches before, and there can be judgment in how teachers perceive coaches, that maybe coaches are teachers who took the easy way out, couldn't keep their hand over the candle.

This is the classic feeling of frontliners for rear echelon troops, a mix of disdain and envy, though in fact, the teachers are half-wondering what it would be like not to wake up sick, thinking about the day ahead. It was tough leaving the school, and some of the students, kids I had fought for years to develop trust with, were angry. I was just another person who had let them down. I didn't like that part of the change.

After taking the job, though, when I was a coach I spent an inordinate amount of time talking about my classroom. I never introduced myself as a coach, but as a teacher, on a two-year assignment coaching. So I was clearly conflicted.

I'd had people visit me in the classroom before. They came in on my prep, expounding a vision of calm, thoughtful teaching practice into the echoing silence of my kid-free classroom—great strategies for learning, for organizing, for vocabulary and for concept transmission. The coaches were wise, they were rational, they were free. When the bell rang, and my 5th and 6th period reading class rolled in cloaked in a chaotic fog of pre-adolescent angst and potential, the coaches packed up their rolling bags and left.

The minute they stepped out my door, the clarity slipped away, and into the space in my head where the new method had floated, the minute-to-minute reality flowed back in—someone's latest unmedicated bipolar outburst, a random phone call from the band teacher looking for a music folder, and three suspensions that left my reading class's Red Group without half of its members, leaving me wondering how I'd fill them in on the Main Idea strategy they were missing.

Sometimes, when the kids were gone, in the 15 minutes a day I had between the last bell and the time I had to go pick up my own kids from school, I'd think about the methods and ideas, and gradually, like a subterranean termite building a mental mud tunnel, begin a very gradual incremental change in my classroom practices. There were a lot of other things to manage, but I did it, over time. It took weeks to try something out, but the bottom line was that if it made my daily teaching life better, I did it.

So when it came time for me to step into people's classrooms, I always remembered what it was like from my side, when I was the teacher entertaining the coach.

For the next couple years, I wandered the district, like a Flying Dutchman with a projector, visiting more than 70 teachers, many several times each. By signing up for the project, the teachers received an LCD projector, a laptop, and a small video camera, and could then use these tech tools to improve their practice. They could also receive a set of small Netbook computers, loaded with software for visual learning and writing support.

My coaching colleague and I (he coached the elementary school teachers) met briefly in the morning, but the rest of the time I was on the road. I got to know the streets of Saint Paul as well as any taxi driver. I had a lap desk, and would pull up outside schools I didn't know so I could pick up district wifi.

I visited middle schools, high schools, schools for teenage moms, jails, and transition centers where kids between 18 and 21 got training in job skills. I walked into dozens of worlds, some as harmonious and functional as my own school, some where my hackles went up and I scanned the hallway, looking at a bunch of kids hanging out after the bell had rung, watching teachers shut the doors on them, leaving them to run the halls. That school was a powder keg waiting to blow up.

I spent time in high schools for students who had just arrived in the US, and had to learn English, lower-level academics and higher-level academics at the same time. Which they did, somehow.

Mostly what I did as a coach was listen. I heard people's stories, tried to reach into their world with hope, suggest new ways to make things better for their kids, and by extension, for themselves. I got to know a lot of other teachers, and experience a little of their lives. Some of them were actually heroes, running good classrooms in schools with no administrative support, where special ed was literally in a basement, kids thrown away because they might bring down test scores. I met teachers in juvenile school, called Boy's Totem Town, who had the least discipline problems of any of us. The boys wanted to go to class, because no matter how much they didn't want to admit it, school was basically the only thing they had to do.

I saw kids there I had known, a couple of years after they had been in my science class, kids already bumping up against the system back then, and now arrived at the kind of outcome we had feared for them. One kid in particular I remembered as high energy, very bright, but confrontational. I was visiting his teacher, talking about vocabulary strategies, and he was in line to enter the class. He saw me, and greeted me like we were old friends. I was glad to see him and told him I'd say hello to Mr. M., my science co-teacher, when I saw him next—I did, and we were both a little sad about how things had turned out for the kid.

It was one of the reasons I thought I should write this book. Two years of visiting gave me a pretty good idea what things were like for the teachers in my district, and it wasn't covered anywhere in the newspaper, heard on the floor of the legislature, discussed around backyard barbeques where people complain about their schools, or listed on agendas in lacquered, dark-paneled rooms where executives decry the failure of schools to provide them with an educated workforce.

Two years, 70 teachers, more than 200 coaching visits in

32 schools, led me to a conclusion. Into the lack of understanding, the ignorance of learning's complexity, and the blind judgment of the world, I have three words for any of the people who complain about teachers.

You try it.

Agencies

A lot of supporting agencies converge around students living in a world close to the poverty line, and I saw them often at my school.

The most visible agents were the police, who had a regular presence at my school. For a few years, before budget cuts increased the number of schools he visited, we had a community resource officer with a small substation, in a room right near the auditorium.

The idea was that he'd get to know the kids, could get out ahead of any larger incidents, and that kids might change their idea of the police as adversaries in the community. I can't say for sure whether that worked, though I know many of my students spent time in police cars, talking their friends into trying to stay out of police cars, or seeing other people getting into police cars.

It was just a different way of life. In the places they lived there were a lot activities going on that resulted in police visits. Was it profiling or harassment? There was definitely some, I heard the stories. I only know what I saw in the schools. We pretty regularly had police officers leading kids away. Not daily, but a few times a year at least. Once we even had federal agents at the school, although I never found out why.

The other main group of agencies were social, and we had a lot of contact with them. Sometimes our social worker would bring in Child and Family Welfare to try to get additional help for a kid, or decide if a kid needed a change in where they lived, or some other Olympian decision I was very glad I had no part in.

For myself, and most teachers in my building, other than the ones who regularly dealt with the most troubled kids, county and community agency people were just another form of Visitor. Someone harrowed-looking, with distant eyes and the air of someone fighting the good fight, walking by with admin, wearing a name tag. I give them credit, they often had caseloads in the hundreds, and no resources whatsoever, but they were still trying to do what they could.

The district sometimes came in with the Agencies. The one you really didn't want coming around was the Office of Civil Rights. For some reason, and I was never quite sure why, we went through an audit, and even had a consultant come in to help us through the audit. The consultant met with a select group of people to be sure we were running our special ed processes properly, and didn't have kids in overly restrictive environments.

Twenty IEPs were randomly chosen to be reviewed, and—lucky me—one of mine was picked. We had to run through it and explain any things I did that were slightly out of alignment, without quite mentioning the Elephant in the Room, which was that if we followed every single one of the regulations to the letter, it would be so time-consuming I'd live at the school and sleep an hour a week.

When that Agency came through there was a cloud of focus, a whiff of fear wafting in with them, drifting down the hallway as they approached.

They stopped briefly through my classroom, which was either an honor (my classroom was chosen as a demonstration room), or a dishonor (suspect in some way, they had red-flagged me and I was not going to be back the next year.) It was neither, just random, actually.

The most regular contact I had with Agencies was through a form we got sometimes, in which we were asked to verify a kid had a disability, so a parent could get additional federal aid called SSI. I was supposed to do it every time, but I didn't.

I filled them out in a couple of cases where the kid's learning disability was profound, and I knew the parents were making a tremendous effort to help, even paying for tutoring they couldn't afford.

Mostly I didn't, since the funds were better used for kids who had truly profound mental and physical challenges. It wasn't my call to make, but I did it anyway. It was through these forms I actually came into contact, the only time in all the years I taught, with an actual Welfare Mother of the type so demonized by the right wing of American politics. She really was trying to exploit the system and was quite irate when I didn't fill out the form. She pressed me, even came to the school, but when it became clear to her not only that I wouldn't sign the form, but if she continued to push, I might tell someone she was trying to get money for a slight learning disability for her kid, she backed off. Hundreds of students over the years, one Welfare Mother. Not exactly an epidemic of people living off the state.

(Non-) snow day

The windows in our house were new, so they never did anything quite as poetic as rattle, but I knew when the storms hit. In a half-awakened dream state, I'd hear the rumbling, skittering crashes of a snowplow scraping down our street. Maybe I'd get up, look at the streetlight, at the swirls of snowflakes drifting earthward in the glow, spinning and whirling, as random as a politician's moral compass.

I'd have an inkling of what was coming the night before as I drove home, listening to the predictions of what my favorite sports radio talk show host called Weather Terrorists. The host would mock the weather people for predicting yet another "snownami," which would either have three or six or 10 inches. The fact of the matter was, it was never as much as I wanted.

Closing schools in a district our size was done only under extreme conditions, because making up a day for 40,000 students and more than 5,000 teachers and staff costs a lot of money. They might do it if the wind chills at the bus stops were guaranteed lethal (one year it was 5 below and we still had school) or there was so much snow the buses couldn't get down the side streets.

So I'd wake up early, knowing I'd need to shovel, or snowblow if it was bad, frowsily donning my Carhartt's insulated coveralls to go out at 5 a.m. to start clearing the driveway. After bashing through the icy berm of the driveway, where the snow had been piled in a crusty wall by the plow, I'd come back in to eat, drink coffee, and hope against hope, checking the websites scrolling the list of school closings.

Our Lady of Blessed Intervention—Owatanna
Hmong Charter Academy—South Saint Paul
Friends School—St Paul
Christ Triumphant Christian Magnet School—Fridley...

Saint Paul Public Schools? Nope. Not today.

Hopes dashed, I'd drag my own kids to school, and head into The Building, to be greeted by near-empty halls, with maybe a quarter of the kids in attendance. Unlike duty-bound teachers and administrators who slid down streets half-filled with snow and ice, the kids, quite sensibly, had stayed home.

Sometimes these days were great. You might find a way to help that really troubled kid in 4th period, or catch up on school news as you stood in tranquil hallways. One thing was sure, the kids who came to school on these days fit one of three categories—they were more than typically dutiful, were kids who wanted to be at school (which they couldn't stand) more than home (which they really couldn't stand), or had parents who were total hard-asses.

The first years, I was at a loss. I had planned on everyone being there every day, so if I went on with the week's plan, half the kids would be way behind. Later, I learned to keep a reserve assignment for non-snow-day snow days, something on topic, but not essential.

We drifted through the day, like the snowflakes that caused the situation, floating to an easy dismissal, halls zombie-apocalypse empty.

Maybe the storm would pick up overnight and we would have a real snow day tomorrow and could stay home. Maybe.

But not likely.

MARCH

Spring break

The mystical significance Spring Break took on for students and teachers went far beyond nine days in March. It was a breakpoint, a watershed, the Rubicon we all crossed on our way to the sacred haze of summer and freedom.

Coming out of the abyss of midwinter, spring break loomed large in our thoughts. The ground was still frozen, snow still very much in evidence, but we knew that at some point, even as we dragged through the frigid air on the way to our cars, someday in the imaginable future it would all get better.

A few kids in my daughter's suburban high school might talk about going somewhere over break, like Mexico, or even Hawaii, but that wasn't really in the cards for my students. Practically speaking, about all they could hope for was maybe a road trip to hang out with cousins in Chicago or St. Cloud, but that wasn't what we all wanted out of the vacation.

Spring Break was, most of all, a chance for It To Stop. For at least five blessed workdays, with a weekend on either side, none of us, students or teachers, would have to place ourselves onto the conveyor belt of the school day and march stiffly through mornings and afternoons of precisely regimented speech and activity. We could do something different, or even—gasp—nothing at all.

Sometimes, during Spring Break (it's always mentally capitalized for a teacher) I would wake up, grab a cup of coffee, and enjoy the insane decadence of just staring out my kitchen window at the snow. Sunlight sparkled through the higher parts of the drifts, which by that time were often four or even five feet tall, since they were near the driveway and that's where all the snow piled up as I used the snow blower.

I knew my garden was under that snow, and relatively soon I'd have access to the soil, and be able to spend my evenings and weekends outside, under blue sky, digging in soil that was at this point still frozen. But at least the days of sun, light, and dirt in my hands were coming.

I realize that for some teachers snow is not a factor in their spring break, but I imagine them staring out the window nonetheless, whether in Memphis or Albuquerque or Honolulu. The point was the ridiculous luxury of simply staring. No one saying your name, no phones, no PA, no bells.

The other interest that kept me sane and helped me make it to the end of school was baseball. A colleague of mine was an equally devoted Twins fan, and we talked a lot of baseball right around Spring Break. Pitchers and catchers had typically reported some weeks before break, and one of the things that kept me going was knowing people were throwing and catching baseballs, on green grass, in the sun, even if my world was still dark and frozen.

By Spring Break, opening day was often near, and if the timing was right, we jacketed up and went to Target Field, seeing spots where the snow had been melted off the diamond, the Twins bundled up to the point where they looked like 1920s football players. Baseball season was a sign that winter would soon be over and we knew we'd be back— to sit in the sun, drink beers and watch grown men get paid hundreds of millions of dollars to play a child's game all though the long, warm summer.

Spring Break could include the kind of Day Counting-Time Awareness that echoed the last days of summer, or the last days of the school year. I'd be careful not to even think about it. (It's Tuesday, I'm not at school.) Push that thought away, because if I didn't, I'd realize there were just three days left in the break. Keep it Zen, keep it No Mind, just be.

School calendars are pretty random in the way vacations are scheduled. Sometimes Spring Breaks last five workdays, sometimes seven—if so, you get a leftover half week. This leads to kids coming back to school hating you, school, and everything else. Or they just don't come back that half week, and you have to start your lesson plans over.

The main thing was knowing that on the other side of break, you were on the downslope, the way out, that if you just put your head down and bulled though the early parts of

April, you'd be in Standardized Test season, and then into May, June and it'd be over.

We were going to make it. We had only to roll along with the system, and we'd make it through another year. Amazing what a week off in March can do for a teacher's soul.

Experience gap

Sometimes, even when we tried to be really conscious of the fact that most of us basically lived in a different world than our students, we would run up against the fact that their life experiences were completely different than ours in ways we could not ever guess.

Once in science, without thinking, I was referencing how planes take off. I could see, a couple sentences in, I was not getting my point across. I thought, of course, maybe not all of the kids had been on an airplane. I switched topics and used another example. Later on, as I visited small lab groups, I asked each table in turn, so nobody would be embarrassed, if they had been on airplane. Out of 30, two kids had. I also asked if they'd ever been to an airport and seen a plane take off. They mostly laughed. Bus station, yes. Of 30, six had ever been to an airport, for any reason.

A couple of times while I was teaching that class, I went home to Hawaii, and made a point of bringing back seashells for the kids. I would buy shell leis, disassemble them, and then offer the individual shells up to kids in each of my classes. I knew for a lot of them that was as close to the sea as they would ever get, mostly because they were in Minnesota, the nearest ocean was 1,200 miles away, and they were unlikely to get there anytime soon.

So when we checked for prior knowledge of the physical world, we stayed close to home. No oceans, no beaches, except the ones at the lakes. We drew heavily on family and friends. A lot of kids had traveled state to state, and many had relatives across the U.S. Typically, if they went somewhere, they drove: from their neighborhood to another neighborhood a lot like it.

I gave an assessment called the Transition Preparation Index, designed to survey which life skills kids had developed. One question asked if a kid had a bank account or a checking account. In seven years of asking that question, no one ever did. Which was not unexpected, since they were mostly 12 or 13 years old. But when I asked what they had done on their last family vacation, in seven years I'd say they typically could only remember one, several years ago. Often they said they'd never been on vacation, and several even asked what that would be like. They'd ask—You go somewhere with your family, and do things? Disney World?

That assessment also included questions about where the kids imagined themselves living, five years from now, 10 years from now. I only heard a couple of times that a kid wanted to own a house. In some of the communities, typically the Hmong kids and Hispanic kids, they would imagine owning a house. Most of the other kids said they'd live in apartments. Owning a house was just not typically a part of their expectations for themselves at 13 years old.

Some kids said they'd live with their parents, which made them different than middle-class kids, since middle-class kids probably expected to buy a house. Much to their parents' chagrin, they were more likely than my students to end up returning home to a guest room or basement, having incurred hundreds of thousands of dollars of college debt.

There were also a lot of things my students knew that I did not. We were reading a story about a kid in the streets at small group, in my reading class, and I went through a passage about someone being shot. I was reading the part where the crowd was reacting to the event by running away frantically, and how the character fell dead in the street, and a couple of the boys snorted with laughter.

I was ready to get on them. "What's so funny about that?" I snapped. They told me, with the crystal ring of experience, that the passage was all wrong. They spoke without hesitation, so I figured they weren't trying to play with me. Sometimes kids would try to exaggerate how rough their lives were, and how street smart they were, especially for white teachers who might tend to believe that everyone lived in gangsterland. But I knew these kids pretty well and was reasonably sure they were being truthful.

One of them, a kid who had a lot of trouble staying in his classes, told me first of all, there was no way the crowd would react that way. "You hear shots," he told me, "you get on the ground and look around. See if they are coming from a car, or the street. If it's a car you're cool. Car's gone, and if you're not shot by then you ain't gonna be. Why you gonna run? The guy could still be shooting." The second boy said, "No way he goes down after he gets shot. How big was that gun? .22? Nine? He's the one who's running."

It wasn't like the book was Dr. Seuss. It was a series of stories about kids in an inner city high school, characters like themselves, written by an author who used to be teacher in a school like mine, so it should have been relatively accurate, but it wasn't.

Other things I learned from students included what it actually feels like to be so hungry that your stomach hurts, what it was like to sleep in a tree because you were homeless and your neighborhood was too dangerous to sleep on the ground, and why Coming Home parties (what you did when someone came back from prison) were usually really small because people getting out of jail weren't used to all the noise and lights and people in a restaurant.

So, who had the experience gap?

Panther pride

My third year In The Building, our new principal had settled in, was comfortable with her transition from AP to The Boss, and had started implementing programs to change the overall flow of the life at the school. One thing she wanted was a consistent set of standards that governed how kids behaved in the school.

We did have a system in place to provide a moral code for the school, called Panther Pride, which included the Three Ps–Punctual, Prepared and Polite. Before she rebooted the effort, we talked about these with the kids sometimes, but there was little consistency, and no way to apply the rubric to anything. She got the program running again.

The major anti-learning forces you contend with in a middle school are not, in fact, academic gaps, but are energy-related. In a middle school, you basically bottle a volcano 14 times a day, (aka, the beginning and the end of every period). Getting kids to class on time, having them ready to work, and providing relatively harmonious classrooms were table stakes if we were really going to give every kid a solid education. Panther Pride was designed to provide a model for kids of how exactly to achieve those three outcomes.

At the beginning of each year, we all received a laminated poster to hang on a wall of our classroom. There was a place for each day of the week, and a grid with columns, within which we could write a number with a dry erase marker. At the beginning of each period, you'd recognize if the kids were Punctual (descriptions varied widely), Prepared (what this meant was changeable, in fact, verging on random) and Polite (wildest variations of all.)

I could see these variations because I had both my own classroom and typically at least one other classroom I was co-teaching in.

The kids, being the world-class, diplomat-grade negotiators they were, immediately sought any kind of chink in the armor of how the Three Ps were handled in each classroom. Their motivation to push the boundaries was powerful, but the innovation of adding recess as a prize defeated them and made the whole thing work. This brilliant formulation on someone's part harnessed the most powerful motivator of all, the desire for the kids to be with each other.

Each week, a random period was chosen, and if that each teacher's class for that period met the Panther Pride total point goal for the week, they would get a recess—typically half a period—either to go outside or go to the gyms, depending on the time of year.

For example, if the goal was 30 points in a week, the kids would have to average six Panther Pride points daily—roughly two per category (Punctual, Prepared, Polite) per day. We knew at the end of the previous week which of the six periods would be eligible for the recess. If Period 3, then, had 30 points in a specified week, on the next Friday they could go. Next week, it would be a different period.

When the announcement was made, the principal would come on the PA and say the names of the periods that had earned the reward. It was like announcing the nominees at an Oscars ceremony, the way the kids waited for it, and whether I told them ahead of time that we made it or not, for them it was the clarion call of freedom when the principal said my class' name.. "Miss Y., H., M., Mr. L., Mr. A., K-C., Miss S...." Sometimes, they even cheered.

There was no better way to witness the cognitive disconnects of the middle school mind than watching Panther Pride point recording at work.

Early in the year, they would stumble in the door somewhere near the time the bell rang. The standard I had was this: be in the door by the time the bell rang. To illustrate that, I would shut the door as the bell rang, and not let a kid in for five minutes afterwards. I wasn't totally rigid about it—if a kid was coming down the hall, within a couple feet of the door, I'd let them in. But once the door was shut, it was shut. Testing the boundaries of this rule, kids always fell into categories.

During passing time, I'd stand in the doorway, one foot in the hall, one foot in the room. That way I could watch the room and the hall at the same time. The doorknob was in my hand. As every kid walked in I'd say hello. Later I found out this was good Teaching Practice, welcoming the kids to the room. I mostly wanted to keep a clear line of sight so nothing happened on either side of the doorway, and they were walking right past me, so why not say good morning?

On the room side, I could see the kids waiting. The Squared Away kids would be in their seat waiting for the bell to ring. Bouncers would be other than where their seat was, but would willingly go back, right as the bell rang. Free Spirits, the ones who were determined to resist all through the day, but not really that hard, needed a reminder, but would be in their seats right after the bell.

Then, coming down the hall, I'd see Finish Line Charlie (or Charlene.) This was the kid who was determined to push the limits with an exactitude that would make a test pilot grant grudging respect, wanting to see exactly how far they could stretch time. This kid would be down the hallway with 30 seconds left, talking to someone, 20 seconds, 10 seconds, then they'd start down the hall. Watching me, doorknob in hand. Five seconds. Maybe it was too much ground to cover? When the bell rang, I leapt into action, closing the door and letting them run past behind me. Sometimes Finish Line Charlie, in the early days, would literally tumble through the door. I'd make them go back, and walk through again, slowly.

I should mention we had automatic tardies for any kid out in the hallway when the bell rang, but I did not handle that. The kids went straight to the office, so we could just get started in class. No referral notes. If the kids were too far out, I'd shut the door, and would hear them outside, knocking. But I wouldn't answer. I'd start up my ritual. After a while the AP would come get them.

This kind of demonstration once or twice was usually enough for most kids. But Finish Line Charlie(lene) still wanted to see how close they could cut it. After a couple of months, they'd usually have it timed so their foot was passing through the door as it closed behind them, a photo finish worthy of any Olympian.

Prepared was the second criteria in Panther Pride. Some teachers went down to the level of In Place, With Pencil, even Seated and Facing Forward. In my classes, they had to have the folder (or my Algebra packet) out in front of them. I used an in-class folder they left in my classroom, in bins marked with their names. That way they couldn't say they forgot their work. When I started each Algebra class, I had them hold up their packets, literally.

The criteria were that if one or two kids weren't ready, that was a 2; if more than three weren't ready, that was a 1. If it was always the same person, I'd tell them that they were personally responsible for us not making the recess. In some cases, I simply wouldn't count them anymore.

I wasn't a dictator about the forgotten pencils either. My favorite tactic for that was to have a box of pencils up front, and ask kids to exchange a shoe for a pencil from the box. I picked up forgotten pencils each day to restock the bin. At the end of class they gave the pencil back, and reclaimed the shoe. They often found this to be embarrassing, and somehow magically procured a pencil from somewhere, rather than use the shoe system.

After we indicated Ready, I'd teach the class. One of the ways I managed in-class chatter was if an individual was talking when I had indicated I needed their attention, I'd put their initials up on the board. If I couldn't figure out who was talking, the whole class would get 30 seconds held on dismissal. Sometimes, early in the year, there would be 1:30 up on the board. I'd give them a chance to earn it back. If anyone flipped out, I'd record that too.

The way I looped it back was at the end of class. I always dismissed the kids from their seats, which meant they had to be in their seats for the last minute or so, and they couldn't leave without us doing Panther Pride. Kids volunteered to have the responsibility of recording class points for the week.

The chosen kid would look out over the class and ask, "Were we Punctual?" At first all the kids would all answer they were, but after they realized I actually kept track of who was late, they'd all yell a number and I would agree or disagree. I kept veto power, but once you established it as a reasonable thing, they never seemed to object, except in a pro forma way. They were not only looking for fairness from me, but were remarkably fair themselves.

"Were we prepared?" They'd think it over. If someone had gone through class with never having materials, I'd point that out, or they would, and so on. Typically, by November, peer pressure had everything flowing smoothly.

The last category was Polite. Many times it was a 2, because there would be 30 seconds on the board. Since I wrote everything down, all I typically had to do was point.

Once in a while, they would try to argue ridiculously. The kid would call out, "Polite?" They'd all say "All 3s!" And I'd say "You kidding?" Then I'd point up at the white board with all the initials on it, running down the litany.

"First of all, Kylie never even made it through the warmup before she had to leave the room. I don't know what's up with her today, but on her way out she definitely was NOT polite. Then, you guys got up to 1:30 today—look at all the initials up there. You brought it back together, but this was not your best day. You still owe me 30 seconds." Scrawled up on the white board, often crooked or even sometimes sideways, since I often wrote with my back to the board, were the initials. DT, TB, K (some kids only needed one name), SM. The kids went along with it, because the evidence was right there. "Okay, 2?," they'd say. Give them credit for effort, future lawyers, maybe. "Nope, 1 today. You'll have a better day tomorrow."

There were some kids who were so unable to regulate themselves that at a certain point I would no longer include them in the system, since the class would never make recess if I included that particular kid, and it actually would have been unfair. However, in that case, that one kid did not get recess if the class earned it. Kids who fell in that category were rarely in class, though.

The period points goal was a sliding scale, so it got harder as the year progressed, and usually it followed a bell curve. The hardest part was the first time the kids didn't make it—when the standard had gone up, they had been making it, but then they didn't. The first time it happened they were pretty irritated, but the standard had to be shown to be real.

On the whole, Panther Pride worked really well. I wish we had it in corporate life. Wait—we do—it's called performance reviews.

Image

My wife was traveling, and at an airport newsstand, she saw a magazine cover featuring an image of a blackboard on which the words "We must fire bad teachers" were written over and over again.

She brought the magazine home, so one weekend when I wasn't grading papers I read the article: it was a barely-informed, one-sided diatribe about teachers holding on to lifetime protection, along with a cartoonish portrayal of national teacher's union leaders. In the article, teachers and unions were said to be resisting accountability as brave district superintendents and reformers fought cliques of lazy teachers hidden in teacher's lounges vowing that legislators would pry tenure from their cold dead fingers, even as their students couldn't pass standardized tests.

Yeah, got it, well done in terms of trope recycling. I was, by no means a blind teacher's union booster, but I've worked in corporate America long enough to appreciate the idea of a contract. I do think the unions are not skilled enough in spinning their side of the story. Begs the question, though: Where do those images (which the article's author only had to touch on briefly to evoke) come from?

Wherever they are coming from, they certainly are widely held. One night at Target Field, one of those mid-inning, hunt down the unwitting fan and make them do something for the camera games was underway. A fan on the

Jumbotron was asked to guess what relief pitcher Jesse Crain would have done for a living if he hadn't made The Show.

The choices were History Teacher, Mechanic, and another job I can't remember. In a row down below and to the right of me in Section 324, a group of men in their mid-20s shouted out their guesses (mostly Mechanic). Some were in Twins gear, but a couple still wore the button-down shirts, with ties loosened, they had worn to the office that day. When Crain's video image stirred to life and he said he would have been a history teacher one of the men called out "Failure!" The others all laughed.

Teachers, almost as a rule, have master's degrees and further graduate education, work in a system crumbling from within due to changing demographics and dwindling funding streams, and are responsible for teaching students who come to school carrying with them a myriad of challenges. Daily, they handle demands and imperatives from literally dozens of directions, and yet they manage to survive, through creativity, dedication, boundless optimism, and the courage of warriors. After 20 years of service, they might be paid about the same as a 24-year old trainee financial analyst. These were my colleagues, urban teachers, "failures."

This group of young guys were also making more money than a teacher ever could—to serve themselves first, their companies when possible and their clients last. They were worthy of respect. And teachers were "failures."

This is the crux of the image problem. Does the trope of the tenure-grubbing teacher, unwilling to take responsibility for failing schools, cause these perceptions? If so, as always, we can ask the question: who profits? Images don't exist for no reason. They are propagated by agents, with agendas.

If you're not born into old wealth, education is the only way to change the pathway of your life. Generations of working people have pulled themselves into the middle class that way. The middle class has pulled itself into the upper-middle. It was education that opened the path for those young upper-middle class guys to congratulate themselves on their ability to thrive in a school system designed for them, specifically, to prosper.

They are prospering. Surprise. I'm sure some of them (but those hide their stories) came to school worrying about food, safety, housing or language barriers. But public education, at least as we have implemented it in the last 50 years, is designed to provide a path for others, who are not English-speaking upper-middle class guys.

So, who are the failures? The teachers, who in every moment of six hours with students and many more each day besides, struggle to keep the path open, and yes, sometimes fail? Or the people who have benefited from the path, who don't feel it's their responsibility to maintain for others?

Most of all, what will the Bad Teacher forces do if they create public education without tenure, teachers fired due to bad standardized test results, corporate-style profit and loss accountability—and the students still struggle? How deep is their commitment to the public path for students who are the newest Americans, the forgotten students of the inner city, students who are born different and struggle with disability? Who will they blame then?

Images are powerful. I think as teachers the first thing we needed to do was tell the other side of the story. Police officers and firefighters put their lives on the line daily and are heroes. Teachers put their hearts and minds on the line every day and are failures.

There's something wrong with that picture.

Early release day

I led kids down the hallway on wooden skis, shared my prior experiences on Career Day, ran Olympic games in the gym, walked through the mud on the side of the creek by the school, and sat in a circle with kids talking about trust.

This wide variety of activities happened on Early Release Days, a result of the requirement that several days a year we schedule a partial school day in order to meet district-required PD mandates. The crazy schedules that resulted, and what the PD was like, I've discussed elsewhere, but early release day programming was one of my favorite things about being in the school.

Often, we'd have a meeting after school the day before the ERD, and activities would be handed out by people who had volunteered to run the day's programming. Sometimes it was our building coach, a very senior teacher who spent most of her time coordinating activities related to school culture and overall cultural programs. Sometimes it was teachers working on their principal's licenses, who would take on managing the day's organization so they could practice and develop school-wide logistics skills.

I enjoyed those days not only because they were a change of pace, but also because I could meet kids other than the ones I usually taught, and do activities that were not so strictly regimented and academic.

The ERDs that happened early in the year often led to kids who would become noted (or notorious) as seventh graders showing their first signs of whatever would eventually distinguish (or extinguish) them. One kid, who I briefly had in my reading class, clearly emerged as a peer leader through the way he guided one event. In this activity, five kids stood on two-by-fours, one under each foot, to which ropes were fastened, one for each hand. They all had to pull at once, alternating sides, to move the boards forward together. No instructions were given, they had to figure out the best way to do it on their own. This kid took on a leadership role, getting the kids to alternate—pulling together on one side, then the other side.

Across the hallway, another kid gave up, jumped off the boards and cursed out the other kids loudly. He also was a seventh grader, and later became a frequent flyer, as kids who spent a lot of time in the principal's office were tagged.

I sometimes wondered if we did these kinds of activities on purpose for the first ERD, and came to believe that even if we didn't, we should.

I'll admit that later in the year, as I was hanging by a thread, coordinating a tricky activity every 30 minutes all morning with a bunch of kids I had never met—and who were every bit as much hanging by a thread as myself—could be quite challenging.

Due to budget cuts, it was one of the only times that kids still got to do art. There were door-decorating contests, kids crafted wall hangings, and sometimes even created full-blown sculptures. These days always made me happy. As school day periods got reduced over time, and the school population grew, the students (especially the ones I taught, whose days were fully programmed with remedials) were finally able to get their hands on some art.

Often there were full-scale auditorium meetings, with guest speakers, or sometimes extraordinary people from within the staff. When we went fully to single-gender classes my third year, I was assigned to the boys' teams, and we had a lot of programming dedicated to understanding what it meant to become a young man.

Our choir teacher—and boys community leader—would play guitar (he was a part-time professional jazz guitarist and bassist) and follow up with some frank conversation, a lot of which spilled over into the classroom afterwards. That year we had some of the best ERDs ever, and I felt there was a serious sense of community that developed as a result.

One frequent speaker was Mr. F., a young staffer who had played football at Notre Dame, then with the New York Giants on a Super Bowl-winning team. He basically walked on air in the eyes of the boys. He got up to talk about discipline and sacrifice, and you could have heard a pin drop, even with close to 400 restless middle school boys in one auditorium. He was a handsome guy, and once at an evening event, when he took the stage to speak, all the young women, most of the middle-aged women, and even some of grandmas were spellbound. He was a go-to guy when we were programming either for the boys or the community.

ERDs were also a rare chance to get out and run around, when the weather was good. Sometimes we'd have games outside, with some sort of theme, or, when we all had creative fatigue, just schedule a recess.

Another event that often happened on ERDs was talent shows, which were great. I loved seeing the kids getting up there and flying their freak flags—from very serious and sometimes talented dance crews, to Hmong and African-American girls singing the latest sappy teen songs, to musicians at the very beginning of their skills. One year, there was a spoken word piece from an amazing eighth grade Hmong student, who fired off a quick-moving, near freestyle poem about dreaming in two tongues. I wonder what became of her sometimes. She had chops.

One of my favorite Talent Show stories was about a seventh grader who was, in self-identification nomenclature, a Little Person. He always seemed completely at ease with himself, despite his difference. At least, he presented himself that way. When he first got to the school, kids who didn't know him looked at him with pity, or unease, or just ignored him, though he had a cadre of buddies and cousins that protected him.

The first time he stood up with his crew, keeping time, waiting his turn to dance in the circle, there was an odd anticipation. What would happen? When he got out in the circle and spun, hopped, roboted and slid, the crowd went wild. The kid could really dance. Of course, why wouldn't he be able to? But everyone had been holding their breath, not wanting to be embarrassed for him, or conversely, waiting

185

their chance to mock him. But he could move. He was the best guy in the crew. The crowd loved it, teachers included. It was awesome.

Along with the hip hop and pop singers, there were always Hmong dancers too, girls in a rainbow of brocade and silk, trained from a very early age in Hmong traditional dance, requiring a degree of flexibility that would make a yogi seem as stiff as I felt after running a triathlon. These girls could, apparently, bend themselves into a perfect circle.

From time to time, there were also Native dances, since the school was a magnet for Native American studies. There was one quiet kid who was in a couple of my classes, somewhat on the margins of the school, bullied a bit, kind of an emotional train wreck. When he took the stage in full Lakota eagle dance regalia, there was another of those expectant pauses. Would the kids laugh and disrespect him?

As soon as the music started he took off, graceful and swift, deft-footed and fast, embodying the wildness, almost like he was an eagle, the song of the drum chanter echoing through the auditorium. He finished, there was a brief hush, then the crowd roared. It turned out he was one of the best Native youth dancers in the Upper Midwest, and a regular on the major powwow circuit, including Sundance in South Dakota, the Super Bowl of Plains Native events. He had a kind of minor rock star status after that, even from the most street-wise kids.

ERDs always seemed a bit like a vacation, in the way that variety can cause a change for the better. I think the kids really liked ERDs, and I definitely always appreciated them.

APRIL

Standardized mess (AKA No Child Left)

Once upon a time, there was perfectly reasonable idea. Because education is regulated by the states, who pay for schools in the form of operating funds drawn from taxpayer money, once a year someone should take a core sample of basic knowledge to see if kids are learning anything.

In its earliest form, when cavemen and dinosaurs roamed the earth in the 1970s, the test was called the Iowa Basic, and it was such an anomaly in my own life as a student I never quite knew what to make of it. The test was a weird thing that happened once in elementary school where we filled in bubbles. Then it happened again in high school. No big deal.

The numbers were seen by a handful of school district officials, kids looked at the numbers and hoped they were good, but there was no earth-shaking significance attached to any of it by the majority of the people involved. The tests certainly were not designed to become the foundation of curriculum for a school.

That was before No Child Left Behind came along.

There aren't any teachers who don't think their work should be measured, let's get that straight right now. Teachers feel accountable for what they do, because futures are at stake. Nobody is dodging responsibility for outcomes. What led to the Tests Gone Wild scenario we face now is the idea that through standardized tests we could finally close the achievement gap between white kids and kids of color (which is also between kids at different socioeconomic levels) and that taxpayer funds should be well-utilized—as defined by the side of the aisle where a legislator sits.

The bill, which came to be called No Child Left Behind, was introduced into a Republican-controlled Congress by new president George W. Bush. The bill, because of the way it was worded, earned bi-partisan support. But federal law does not directly regulate education. That responsibility lies with individual states and independent school districts. So a bill has to be what is termed "operationalized," sent out to each state and verified, which then determines how it will be implemented.

Federal funding is released into school systems only when certain conditions have been met. This includes funding for reading and special ed, without which most districts can't operate.

So No Child Left Behind, operationalized, came to take on a form no one expected—the very aspirational goal that by the 2013-2014 school year, 100 percent of all students would be proficient on standardized tests.

Warning lights go on. Get more kids to a place where they are proficient, sure. But when working with our students, so many factors come into play to affect their proficiency that getting to 100 percent was ludicrous. Everyone was willing to take a shot at 99 percent, but that wasn't the way the law was operationalized—the standard was 100 percent.

Even when the most severe and profound kids with mental and physical challenges were ruled out, and when groups of kids that couldn't read or were English language learners were not considered, in a district our size we were talking about thousands of kids taking a test that was a challenge like no other they faced.

The tests, although efforts were made to change them to be socioeconomically neutral, still included items biased against poor kids and kids of color.

I remember one standardized math test with a question about catering. I was proctoring a room full of kids. A student raised his hand and asked me, "What's catering?" I couldn't tell him, according to the rules. The chances this kid had been to a catered event were the same as him sitting down on the couch to play XBox with Barack Obama.

Once the 100 percent bar was set, they added an extra stick to the carrot, which wasn't even an optional carrot. They added a baseball bat, in fact.

Each school would have a number of kids judged proficient on the test, in Math and Reading. Each year the school would have to make progress at a certain rate, adding to that proficient pool. If they made progress they were fine. If they did not, there was a two-year period termed Safe Harbor. After that, if the numbers didn't go up, the school went on the Non-Performing List.

The List was comprised of schools that did not meet growth targets. The first year on the List, a school got extra help. The second year, more scrutiny and less help. The Federal government actually started to reduce funding. The third year, further funding was withdrawn, and the school housed full-time staff in place to monitor compliance. The fourth year, a school was administered by outsiders, working from a plan designed to save the school. More money was removed, programs cut, and the school became a reading and math factory. The last year, if the school didn't make the numbers, it was disbanded, kids and teachers distributed to other schools in the system. The term death spiral comes to mind.

Also, as the tests became more high-stakes, the effects were manifold. Their frequency increased, so kids were taking tests more often. By the time I left they took one almost every year between 3d grade and 11th grade. Second, the variety of tests exploded. There were not only standardized tests for all students, but additional tests specifically for English language learners and special ed kids. Many took both, or even all. The month of April became a long series of tests. Third, the tests themselves were unlike anything anyone ever did in school.

There was a huge emphasis placed on test prep, on reading items, breaking down items and details of the test. By my last years, there was an additional science test.

The tests lasted for hours, in a school where our assessment philosophy was focused on short knowledge checks and quick hands-on testing, leading to a 52-minute long chapter test. All of a sudden, we asked kids to sit down and read, write, do math and also remain completely silent for three hours?

They never did anything for three hours. If we were serious about it, we would have trained them like athletes, running up from one, to two, to three hours. But what would happen to the rest of the curriculum then? What happens to the teaching?

The standardized science test was a good indicator. One year we had an 85 percent pass rate in our science class, which we taught very strictly synchronized with the state standards. Every lesson connected to a standard, every test item connected to a standard, yet somehow when they took the standardized science test we had a proficiency rate of less than 50. We knew the kids, we had evidence galore that the test was inaccurate, but when the results came back, we still felt bad, and so did they.

Kids and teachers also tried to ascribe a reason to something that didn't really have a reason. The kids would ask if they had to pass the test to get to 8th grade, or get to high school. Sometimes we'd say yes. Or a kind of yes. Teachers tried to find a reason for the test when talking to each other as well. It will be a check on our progress, it will be a good core sample, it will be...something?

But it wasn't, really. Districts tried to find ways around

the death spiral. There were ways kids could be tested alternatively. The biggest question was, which kids really required the alternate tests?

One year we received mixed guidance. For three years, I coordinated alternative testing for my school, scheduling all the kids who had IEPs to take an alternative test, when appropriate. There were district meetings where we got guidance on which kids should take the tests, and which kids shouldn't.

So I made the lists, with input from all the other special ed teachers. But there had been a tremendous breakdown in communication somewhere. That year, many kids I thought were supposed to take the alternative test were not, even though they had taken the same test the year before. The area special ed superintendent, when she discovered who had taken the tests, flipped out. She believed I had defied her, and had kids take the alternative test through some agenda of my own. In a very unpleasant meeting, the special ed super threw me under the bus, with a formal warning.

The reason—it looked bad for the district to have too many alternates. It looked like we were trying to get too many kids out of taking a test that actually had no meaning for them. Though I hadn't intentionally defined policy, in the end I was comfortable with what I did. Giving a three-hour sit down test to a kid with ADHD does not tell you what they know. Period.

The funny thing is that 2013-2014 school year has come and gone. Near the end of NCLB, suburban schools in high property tax districts realized they wouldn't be able to make

99 percent (they had started at 92 percent back in 2005, and just never had to worry about the number until later), and NCLB magically melted away, as districts and whole states opted out. What it meant to the kids who lived through the 2004-2012 school years in districts with poorer kids will not be seen for a while, but it has to have affected their prospects over the longer term.

Superstars and dead weight

Everyone—kids, the staff, admin, other teachers—knew who the excellent teachers were, and by extension, who they weren't. Nothing was said, overtly, but you could tell whose classes the kids liked to go to, who the staff looked up to, and who the kids avoided. Sometimes excellent teachers were formally recognized, but the terrible teachers were very rarely called out.

The dynamic behind all this hidden judgment and a reluctance to call people out either for good or ill, was a kind of crab bucket (if you climb to the top of the heap a bit, don't try to climb out, others will pull you back in) mentality. It was important to be a good teacher, one who earned respect from your colleagues and from the kids, but you didn't want to be too excellent, since by extension that was a commentary on your peers.

The I Rule My Classroom as A Kingdom dynamic allowed people to do basically whatever they wanted once the door closed. But from time to time, some event would point out what was going seriously right—or wrong.

In the case of right, it was the metrics from my co-taught science classroom which showed 85 percent of the kids passing, including kids passing that class who failed everything else. I am overly proud of that and have mentioned it before, but so be it. It took a lot of teamwork to get to that point.

My co-teacher in that class won the Presidential Science Teacher award, but he was so well-liked it didn't impact him with the kids or with staff. A couple of other times, when we had someone who had been a Teacher of the Year or some other kind of honoree transfer to our school, there was suspicion: Who is this person? How far out did they put themselves to get this? As though it was somehow self-aggrandizing to seek excellence.

The converse was shown once, when we looked at a report about how many times we kicked kids out of class. I was relatively low on the list, not like it never happened, and of course there were some cases I could have handled differently.

But one teacher, and our names were deleted (although everyone knew who it was) had dozens of referrals in first semester alone. By contrast, I had a total of 15 referrals over the same period of time.

Sometimes I'd talk to kids who came out of that class, after having been kicked out. "I don't even know what I did," they'd say. One kid said, "She didn't like the way I didn't say anything." That was an example of completely dictatorial (and thus, ineffective) classroom management.

Another example was that of a co-teacher I had one year. I had never heard anything bad about his/her classes (I am still reluctant for anyone to know who it was, since I expect some of my old colleagues might read this.). I could sometimes hear this teacher's classes through the door as I passed by, but I attributed the sound level to engagement and the general rowdiness level of seventh-grade boys. I knew the teacher, and to me that person seemed like a solid practitioner, no indicators that that classroom was anything less than typical. Until late one year, when I was assigned to co-teach with the person.

When I got into the class, I discovered that the inmates were running the asylum. The most basic behavior management rules were in place, but beyond that was chaos and rage. I couldn't believe the fact that the kids got away with behavior I'd consider completely out of control. I knew in that class it would be difficult to stand in front of the class as a co-teacher, as I did elsewhere. So I didn't.

I never mentioned what was happening in that class to anyone. I should have, and knew the kids were not being well served, but the pressure on teachers not to rat each other out is significant, and I lacked the moral courage to talk to anyone about it. I did what I could to change what happened in class, for individual kids, but I still fault myself for not doing more.

As a co-teacher, I saw a whole range of other people's styles. Most teachers were quite functional, things ran well, they liked the kids, the kids liked them, and the work got done. Occasionally I taught with people who were operating on another plane: masters and mistresses of their craft.

Although the ways we knew a teacher was good were many, very few are quantifiable, so there wasn't a lot of recognition. But in that carefully egalitarian world, you could tell the difference between respected and disrespected teachers when they spoke in large groups, such as PD. Some were heeded, some were tolerated, and a couple, not up to standard, but carried along inside the body of the school like a parasite, were ignored.

The respected teachers tended to be placed where they could lead peers, on committees, study groups and the like. I have no idea where I fell in that spectrum of respect. I suppose I was doing ok, since the kids didn't avoid my classes, and I was able to contribute frequently enough in large group discussions. It was something I never really thought about.

The bottom line problem with the crab bucket, though, was from a kid's point of view. The only thing people who impact lives—whether it's life and death; like doctors or firefighters; or simply long-term outcomes, like teachers— should be is excellent. People being people, that's just not how it works. That's not right for the kids who survive through the classes of people who should really be doing something else with their working lives.

Methodology

As a school struggling with test results and what were deemed underachieving students by dint of their test scores, we were fertile ground for people who wanted to unleash the latest and greatest in teaching methodologies.

As an eager first-year and early-tenure teacher, I didn't understand the skepticism of the older teachers as we trained in yet another vocabulary, critical thinking, or professional development strategy. The seasoned folks just shrugged. This too shall pass, they said, though they adopted the methods anyway.

We would typically be introduced to the idea in large-scale PD, often trained by the person who designed the methodology in the first place, eventually receiving a huge shrink-wrapped package in the mail. We read the books and manuals, and tried, at least most of us, to use the New Method. Every one was Research-Based, designed to Improve Achievement (aka test scores), and Improve Outcomes for Kids.

Each of them had likely done that, for the professors who developed them in single or small groups of classrooms, over a period of years, and who used only that method. Each of them certainly also Improved Outcomes for someone's revenue stream, since they were usually very expensive. When, over time, they did not work the same in the hundreds of classrooms as they had in the few, the blame was often placed on teachers, who had implemented with a "lack of fidelity."

Fidelity meant doing the same thing the same way every single time, which might be feasible in a research classroom. They were classrooms in a school where the professor had spent years with the same teacher implementing the methods, and often times they worked. The ironic aspect to me was that the the researchers granted themselves something we did not get—continuity. When they practiced their methods over and over, there was no one to ask them to use another new method the next year, and the next, and the next. They also didn't have three preps, six periods and 25 IEPs.

With such a small group of kids, you could have something that met research fidelity standards. You could tweak and refine and hone and revise, trying it over and over again, which we could not, since we were just trying to run the machine, keep the kids from yelling at each other, and teach.

The other major gap was in the administration at the district level, who would roll these out, then think everyone was still doing the method forever, often without ever checking back to see if we were. After the second year after rollout, there would be no more talk of the New Method. So out in the classrooms we would ask ourselves and each other—are we still supposed to be doing X? Are we still supposed to be looking at the wall, pointing at the Accountable Talk phrase, checking fluency three times a year with the SRI? We didn't know. Sometimes we would ask at

Child Study, and get a shocked reaction from district people—you mean, you're not still doing that test? We'd say, well, nobody mentioned we were supposed to keep doing that test, and it overlaps with the new test. So we stopped.

The scripted nature of some of the classroom work was humorous, since to implement with fidelity I had to follow word for word—as a seventh-grade girl cried about a breakup, as I kept two kids from throwing things at each other, as I realized that suddenly none of my dry erase markers worked, as I dealt with fire drill, intruder drill, Panther Pride recess period, power loss, snowstorm that left no buses running and three kids in class.

Following the script to the letter doesn't always help a kid with a wounded heart, because all the methods in the world can't change the fact that her mom is a drug addict who left her in an abandoned building with 20 bucks to feed the family, and she is so mad he can't see straight.

There are very few vocab methods that can get a kid to focus when he's about to meet his dad for the first time in his life; or when a beloved grandmother, who raised a kid since her mom was in another state, has just died; or when a girl who never thought anyone would like her has a first boyfriend. No rubric for that, no method to get you through, just time and belief and even, in a way, love.

I actually think that is the way it is supposed to be. Kids are a marvelous mishmash of personalities. A classroom is not an operating room, or a science lab, it is filled with people, in my case people nowhere near fully-formed. So it makes sense there's a middle ground that develops between our own practice and what is dictated by the Method. This is anathema to the people who sell the Methods, and the people who buy the Methods. They worship validity with the fanaticism of a temple acolyte.

One day I heard a radio show about a British physicist named John Polkinghorne, one of the originators of string theory, who later became an Anglican priest. He said the Clockwork view of the universe holds that the universe is a machine, the Cloud model of the universe is embodied by chaos theory, and that we live somewhere in between.

I couldn't agree more, and I think teaching is like that. You need to have purpose and method, structure and rhythm, but also allow each kid to be unique in all the world, in both their resources and challenges. Reading is complex, nuanced and mobile, and the true nature of comprehension is the holy grail of reading. Math is numerology and numerical at once. Science is fact, but also mystery and magic and an eternal seeking for truth.

Most of all, kids are not widgets we can quality control. Method is a fine servant, but a terrible master.

Scar tissue

(This essay is unfinished. I've tried several times to go back to my memories of these and other kids, but after a while I don't want to. So this is all I'll write on the subject.)

It builds up slowly over the years, around your heart, as you hear the stories. They are stories that don't typically happen to someone like you, to kids like your own kids, coming from families like your own families.

At first they all hurt, but sadly enough, over time, you are no longer surprised, until there is something new, and that strikes you hardest, when the story finds a part of your heart you have thus far avoided scarring. Then it hurts twice as bad. We don't talk about the stories at home with our spouses and families. After a while, even talking about it doesn't change how you feel, so we just carry them.

Unbreakable

A student in one class was shorter than usual because he was malnourished—unfed, basically—and lived in a closet, while his mom, a drug-addicted prostitute, worked in the next room. When he finally got into foster care, at the age of five he was barely three feet tall and weighed less than 40 pounds. This kid taught himself to read so well in my class, going from second to seventh grade level, that he made National Junior Honor Society by eighth grade.

Belief System

A kid showed up at school about a month into the year. He was an eighth grader, tough kid, a little burly for his age, and he soon became a topic of conversation in the teacher's lounge. I saw him in algebra, which that year I was co-teaching with a veteran teacher. The kid seemed bright enough, but basically refused to do any work at all. Not tremendously defiant, but firmly. He said he had no need of an education, since he was going to be employed by his father's landscaping business as soon as he was able to quit school. The work refusal became a significant problem for the kid, but he was adamant. My science co-teacher also had the kid, but in a different period than the one I co-taught, and he was the only teacher able to get any work out of the kid. Even then, it wasn't much, and it was sporadic. No need to do anything, the kid said, soon I'll be working for my father. The admins tried to contact people listed as family, and over time, the truth emerged. When the social worker finally contacted an aunt, after the mother didn't return any calls, the aunt told us the kid's mother was more than a little crazy. "His father?" the aunt said. "He's never even met his father." Kid moved, again, before April.

Lunch Line

Kid was a seventh-grade girl, often troublesome, seriously so, taught by her mother to smile in the face of any reproach, which just got her into more trouble. She fought, she talked back, she cried at odd times. She was suspended all the time. One day in the middle of a suspension she came to school. We were surprised. We thought, she hates the place, why would she come here? She told us, "It's the only place I can get food." When the social worker followed up with a home visit, she found the student was the oldest of five kids, living in an abandoned, unheated house. Her mother left 20 dollars for food and disappeared. She was hungry because she used the 20 to buy food for her siblings.

Thicker Than Water

Kid was a funny, charming 7th grader, with an odd inability to sit still and towering rages at unexpected times. I got to know him over the two years, had him in three classes a day. Seemed ok, not the best success story, but just fine. All of a sudden in spring of 8th grade he just disintegrated. I went to talk to the social worker, and asked her what was going on. She asked if I really wanted to know, since I didn't have to. But I cared about the kid, really liked him. She asked again. She knew this would be one I'd carry. I told her I wanted to know. She told me the kid was sexually abused by a family member, who might be back at home, living with the kid's mom. Kid has nowhere else to go, so now is in the house again with his abuser. The kid never quite gets back on track by the time I see him graduate.

Treehouse

I heard a story once from a teacher I met at Boys Totem Town, our district's juvenile corrections school. There was a kid who ended up there repeatedly for minor offenses, so she finally asked him why he kept coming back. The kid said he had been living in a tree in his neighborhood, since he was homeless and it was not safe on the ground. Then he figured out if he got arrested for just the right crimes he could come back and sleep where he would be safe. This kid made it through the juvenile corrections system, somehow later got a GED, and was in college when she told me about him.

There are many more, but I don't like to remember them.

This is a drill

Typically, once I had established a rhythm in the classroom, I was pretty low-key. The kids knew the lines they were supposed to operate within, and mostly stayed there. That's why my reaction to intruder drills typically caught them by surprise. I was absolutely all-business about the drills, and treated every one like there was someone in the hallway coming to kill us.

The reason why is pretty obvious. Between 1980 and the last year I taught, there were 137 school shootings, with 297 students, staff and law enforcement people killed or injured. Depending on your source, there are roughly 98,000 public schools in the US. The odds were low, but that wouldn't change anything if the next school happened to be my school, the next dead students were mine, and the next dead teacher was me. Then the odds didn't matter.

Sometimes we knew there was going to be a drill, just not when. The procedure was that the PA would announce, "Lockdown, intruder in the building." Any kids who happened to be in the hall I would tell to get into my classroom, right now. I'd get some random kid who had been going to the bathroom, or the office, and who didn't know anyone in the room. I'd go and lock the door, turn off the lights and sit by the door. I'd tell the kids to get down on the floor, farthest away from the door. The random hallway kid would sit off alone a little.

At first they might giggle, and some might pretend they were going to play around, but I would tell them the first kid who made any kind of sound, at all, was going to see the AP as soon as the drill was over, no appeals and I'm not kidding. I'd tell them that while they were here, their safety was my responsibility, and their families trusted us to take care of them, so do not speak—as of right now. I told them whoever came through that door would have to go around me. I didn't know what I would do, but I would try to do something.

They were not used to that kind of intensity level from me, but whatever I sounded like, it worked. We would sit, in the near-dark. There would be some light coming through the heavy construction paper we used to cover the door window, so an intruder could not see into the room.

There would be quiet. After a time, someone would yank on the door handle. Hard. Since the AP was 6'5" and his football playing weight at North Dakota State was 250, that was pretty hard indeed.

After a time, the PA would sound the all clear, and we would go back to our business. That was the most serious of the drills. There was another one, Intruder Nearby, where we kept the lights on, but locked the door. That one tended not to be a big deal, and I didn't do my speech.

The weirdest version of this drill ever, was when it was not a drill, and we didn't know why. It was late one day, mid-last period, when they called an Intruder Nearby drill. We could tell it was a real drill because of the timing, right in the middle of the last period, right before dismissal, so if we missed our window with the buses, we'd have 800 kids with no way to get home.

I locked the door and called one of my buddies in a nearby room. What's up? No clue? We going to be able to dismiss? Hope so, I don't want to sit here forever with these guys.

The kids knew, like forest animals around a wildfire, that something was wrong. We finished the lesson. Period over. PA comes on. "Teachers, do not dismiss your students."

Ok, wow. Waiting. Kids getting antsy to leave. One kid told me if he missed basketball practice he'd sue the school. I went to my laptop, went to the school website, and gave him the phone number for the Saint Paul Schools Legal office. He laughed, said he was just playing.

Finally, the PA came on again. "Teachers, you may dismiss." I let the kids out by rows, so they wouldn't clog the doorway. Chaos in the hall. PA came on, "Buses will not leave until all students who usually ride them are aboard." Our little world, almost unhinged.

When all the kids were gone, we gathered in the commons, a big area under the main stairs. Lanyards jingling, coffee hot, water bottles dangling from a finger. The principal came out and said, "OK guys, here's the deal. There was a bear sighted running across the athletic fields, through the staff lot and into the woods down by the creek." This proclamation was met with an outburst of laughter. Of all the scenarios we could ever imagine—gang warfare, enraged student, enraged parent, domestic violence, police standoff, bomb threat, the cause instead was the most lost bear in Minnesota history.

On the other hand, fire drills, though disruptive, were great. We were required to have a certain number each year, so we held them in early fall and late spring, since it clearly would have been foolish in the middle of a Minnesota winter. We'd file out of the classroom, heads assaulted by the fire alarm—still the single loudest sound I have ever actually heard–filling my whole skull with a pulsing shriek as we filed outside to stand in the cool air of fall, or the warm air of near-summer.

The kids liked fire drills since they knew that whatever was happening in class was thoroughly disrupted for that day, and they could see their friends for a couple minutes. The difference between the pleasant holiday nature of the drills and what we'd really do if the building was aflame, filled with smoke, 800 kids were outside and it was mid-February was simply a place my mind didn't go. That was a principal-sized problem, and I was merely a teacher, standing in the sun.

MAY

The end of knowledge

When I was a kid, growing up in a sugar plantation town in Hawaii, on a barely-paved road, the ocean on one side and sugar cane on the other, I knew where to get information. I could ask my parents, read a book, ask a teacher, or ride my bike three miles to the Waialua Public Library, right by the sugar mill, and ask Mrs. Terukina. If she didn't have that information, then I didn't either. For mass media, there was AM radio, and the fuzzy signal of KGMB Channel 9 in Honolulu, which in the days before cable TV just barely reached the North Shore of Oahu, providing us with a narrow stream of other information.

So for me there was true utility in becoming a person who collected a lot of information: books, documents, education, memories. Because if the sources I mentioned above didn't have what I wanted, it simply wasn't there. My mind was starving. If I was interested in the Civil War, there was a book or two in the library, but not many, because in

Waialua, the Civil War was as exotic a subject as Kamehameha's campaign to unify the islands would have been in Mississippi.

At that time (the mid-1970s) the amount of knowledge we now have access to—past, present and future, all facts possible (correct and incorrect), images, video, primary sources, other states, nations, continents, planets—would simply have been impossible to grasp for the 11-year-old Chris.

Many people have written on the change in the nature of knowledge. In education, though, the legacy of the information repository paradigm affects every aspect of a school year: pacing, culture, teaching kids at risk and even the question of whether public schools can prepare a child to be a 21st century adult.

This is how my history illuminates something about the school where I worked. In the early 21st century, the idea of a classroom teacher as sole repository of knowledge on a single subject, in a single classroom, was still an iconic and unaltered one. Kids routinely used their smart phones to instantly find song lyrics on the Net (anyone old enough to remember playing the vinyl, over and over again, picking up the needle, and scrawling lyrics in a spiral notebook?) but still believed their science teacher (along with their textbook) to be the single source on earth for information on galaxies, air pressure or tornadoes.

Other adults, be they special education teachers, homeroom teachers, or support staff, needed to prove to students that we too knew about science, math or geography.

Not that the classroom teacher wanted it that way: if students realized how they could verify and augment their own learning it would create a depth and richness to their education a single teacher and textbook could not match. We needed to directly instruct them in the concept of one student to many sources of information. The Internet and the knowledge it provides also blow the single-repository model out of the water. It allows a truly one-to-many relationship of a subject to its sources of knowledge.

I think this has both advantages and dangers. The dangers are clear: textbooks are carefully written and edited for clarity and accuracy, though with the recent growth of state textbook standards allowing the inclusion of intelligent design and redactive history it's no longer possible to say they are always objective. History in particular has always suffered from political omission: science and other subjects are now undergoing the same fate.

But the proliferation of other information sources is the antidote to the illness of ideological influence designed to provide students with a limited subset of selected facts. The dilution of textbooks, the conquest of school boards by interest groups, and the limits of the single teacher/textbook model together provide a path to follow, which is this: I think teachers must, consciously and carefully, teach kids thinking as a skill, with the same rigor and accountability they use now to teach any other subject.

They should just give kids any background information required—no more memorizing vocabulary words—then provide them with a curriculum that forces them to synthesize, analyze, compare, evaluate. Entire occupations are becoming commoditized by outsourcing, and offshoring and internet applications have eliminated monopolies on procedural knowledge and process completion.

If teachers don't want public schools to produce kids suited only to become an underclass (and there are no teachers that I know who do), they have to break the box, use all the technologies and information they can provide. Some information is junk, but it always has been. Schools now have the opportunity to guide kids through the process of becoming discerning consumers of thoughts, ideas, proposals, ideologies—before they leave.

Teachers can not only level the playing field once and for all, but change the game of public education permanently. They can't afford to operate as a factory, producing industrialized minds. That paradigm lies in rust. Educators need to bring the world to kids, that they may face it, develop the skills to manage it, and have a chance to prosper in a world without informational horizons. If they don't, teachers could be riding school systems down into obsolescence.

Love

I t is heresy to suggest, and will not be acknowledged in any educational journal, newspaper article or email from district administration, but it is true—the foundation of public education is love.

Love is the only explanation for the fact that people return to a school, year after year, to step into a maelstrom of pressure, joy, expectation, tedious drudgery, mind-numbing routine, and moments of wild inspiration.

Love is what drives people to spend hundreds of dollars of their own money on school supplies, to have tough conversations with kids who may never let them know the value of the outcome, for taking grad school classes at night when they are already exhausted because they want to get better at their jobs.

It is the force that holds a classroom together day after day, the kind of commitment that binds the people in a family, better or worse, day-in, day-out, through holidays and weeks of sameness, and seasons of the year.

You can feel it in the staff room, the classrooms, the office and the hallways.

You can feel it through the kids. They will attach to someone not of their family as a guide and patron in the world, and along with their parents, or the person who is their caretaker, find a way towards some kind of success, or reconciliation, at least, in life.

For those people who think teachers are in a classroom because it is a secure job, I suggest a casual glance at the newspaper of any town with a population greater than 100. Even people with 20 years tenure think about leaving sometimes, because they are smart, the pay is low, and despite all the years served, they may or may not have a pension. People who get into it for the summers off and the security don't stay (and shouldn't), because those are not real reasons to come back. While you are In the Building, it is compassion, caring, and hope that keep you in the game. Sometimes, even that is not enough. Despite the love, many people leave anyway, and there are many more ex-teachers than teachers.

You can't quantify it, it doesn't end up in test results, but love explains how the whole magnificent, unstable construct moves. It is the engine, the nuclear reactor that powers hundreds of people, all trying to do the most magical thing there is—take a kid's mind, in need of knowledge and skills, guidance and counsel, and form it into the one asset that can't be taken away, in a world where everything else is up for grabs. Once, an English teacher told she taught her kids that every vocabulary word they learned belonged to them—and them alone—to own and use as only they decided. That was the kind of gift we had to offer.

Love was something everyone had to give, woven within and around both the visible and invisible structures of our school: budget, staff, energy consumption, food consumption, books, computers, pencils, transportation, conflict, fear, growth, achievement—love was the bedrock of it all.

I never asked anyone what they thought about this idea, though. I thought maybe no one would be comfortable admitting it. I wasn't. But I think we all knew it was true.

Budget cuts

By the time I was fourth-year, I knew when to start making calculations. Spring Break was done, standardized tests were underway, and we started thinking, at least a little bit, about next year—and budget cuts.

Through the newspaper, ironically enough sometime after the annual ad that thanked the district's teachers by putting all our names in the paper, would come the latest news about the district's budget shortfall, and speculation about how many people would be gone next year would begin.

The first round of budget cuts led to a switch from the seven-period day to six, with the departure of elective teachers and of programs that motivated kids to go to school for something other than reading, writing and math. Drama and orchestra (I knew a guy who had to cover eight schools— unless he suddenly discovered an eight-day week, I wasn't sure how he'd achieve that) were the first to go.

Then cuts were made in support staff, later replaced by AmeriCorps volunteers, who had, along with the virtue of their volunteering sprit, the ultimate price tag of free. The cuts in aides always hurt—less hands in the classroom, more trips to the AP, rather than out in the hall to talk things over. Those hurt the kids very badly.

There were also cuts in facilities. Late one year, I found

out my beloved portables were being sent to another school. Not that we had the room. The biggest budget-driven change came relatively swiftly. A nearby middle school, small but with a very proud staff and a solid record of achievement for their kids, was going to be closed, and the two schools were going to become one. We would go from a comfortable 650 students to a chock-full 950, teachers on carts, classes in the halls.

There was always speculation about which languages would be cut. First French, then Ojibwa, finally down to Spanish. Which other arts? None left but choir and band. Which after school programs? None left, but somehow we managed to grant fund some of them.

Which people? First-years were gone, some people retired, others moved away from the school. Some people left teaching, to be forest rangers, to be dental office managers, to work at software companies.

The school was like a woman who'd had too much plastic surgery. Basically the same at first, but after a while, so many changes as to be unrecognizable. It was what it was, but it sometimes led to the flight of kids to charter schools, or suburban schools, or remain if they had no other options.

For some reason, my ideas that we use the school for a reality show and take a cut of the ad revenue to fund our programs; or get a major corporate sponsor, change the school name to 3M Middle School, like they do with stadiums; or we wear polo shirts covered with ads, like stock car drivers or golfers, met with deaf ears. Also, nobody went along with my "Let's all buy lottery tickets with some of our salary" proposal either.

The fact of the matter was, it was going to be a challenge to keep the school from eroding over time, like so many others, until some miracle of public policy changed where we got our money. Maybe we open a Starbucks in the Commons?

Field trip time (End of the line)

In May, my lesson planning internal monologue sounded like this: "Monday I want to start Chapter 15. But that's College Fair, so I'll be missing half the kids. I'll start Tuesday, but Wednesday is a half-day because of African-American Community Assembly, and so most of the boys will be gone. Thursday is an Early Release Day, there's a dance, and Friday I'll have a quiz. I've got about a day and a half."

Beyond all that, numerous small field trips filled the last days. The bell rang, I walked in from the hallway to get rolling, and saw maybe three students out of 22. Where was everyone? The kids told me it's Cinco De Mayo, so some kids are at that; also the Service Learning picnic day, so some other kids were gone; six kids from the Mentor Program went to see a baseball game; the Student Council people were electing their officers for next year; all the girls went to the Girl Power assembly, and two boys were suspended since they're so sick of school they threw food all over the cafeteria and got two days. I have the three remaining students pull up their desks and say, "So, remember when I said we could talk about the possibility of life on other planets some other time? I think today is good."

And how long O Lord, how long? Not few enough days to release the Gulag-like grip I have on the students. But soon enough to start the small, penciled-in countdown I kept in the corner of my planner. Small, because I didn't want anyone to know I was counting down the days.

With the end in sight, students and teachers developed a rush of good feeling. Kids who used to tell me daily they hated me and the school and would greet my questions with "Shut up talking to me!" now hugged everyone and greeted me with a big smile and "What's up?" By the last week, I had convinced myself that movies and pizza parties, were, in fact, pedagogically sound.

The last couple days marked the Breathing Out. On the second to last day, the whole population of the school walked a quarter mile away to a huge public park for a picnic. The idea that the long sweet summer lay on the other side of one more day—our epic field trip to a local amusement park called Valleyfair—seemed impossible.

The dust was settling, the pace of our lives slowing down, and like a motorboat when you suddenly cut the throttle, I felt my mind swerve, and slosh around, and finally settle deeper as I decelerated. Sometimes I'd have long talks with people. Sometimes I found I couldn't have long talks. I was so used to burst communicating in the four minutes between classes that at three minutes and 50 seconds, I'd suddenly stop talking.

Day zero. Valleyfair Day. I had a student once who was so obsessed with the end of the year trip it was all he talked about for a month. He drew roller coasters, he drew water parks, so I made all his math problems have something to do with Valleyfair. It was the only day in the year he cared about.

I'd check my kids against the list three times before we left, so I didn't drive away in a bus without a kid, then discover when we got there the kid seemed to be gone, because I thought they rode out, but they didn't.

Once we got to the park we were on our own. There was one teacher, an ex-Marine, who was legendary for leaving the parking lot at high speed to find a bench. "I need to read a book," he'd say. "And this is my only chance, since all summer I'll be taking care of my kids." My buddy T., when he was still at the school, would have a huge flock of kids following him, wanting to take rides with him, and he was delighted. He was in his element.

I'd find a couple of teachers to walk around with, and sometimes a stray kid would join us for a while, just so they weren't by themselves. Kids made out in front of us, overjoyed we could not tell them to stop. Sometimes we'd just look at them blankly, until they got embarrassed and slunk away, then started giggling. They knew, as we did, that soon they'd be free. They'd run by, soaked from the water park, soaked in sweat, high on sugar. Just happy.

Last roll call, sun going down, back into the bus, whose destination was not only the school, but summer. My final fear was that I'd leave someone's kid there, way out in the southeast Metro area, that we'd be rolling back, drowsy, and some kid would say, "Where's LaShay? Hey teacher (I typically didn't know the kids I was responsible for) where's that girl LaShay?" Trapped by my knees between the narrow benches, I'd swivel painfully, frantically trying to figure out what to do. Turn around? Stop the bus? It never happened, but I thought about it.

Off the bus, watching the kids and buses flow away. Into

the office, dropping off the bus attendance sheet, and down the quiet halls into my classroom. Turn off the lights, grab the backpack, and hard as it was to believe, another year was over. The next day would be the farewell breakfast, room cleanup, and for some people, move prep. But I was done.

As of the time I turned my key in the ignition, it was summer.

JUNE

185

The last day. The Building was empty of kids, and teachers gathered in the hallways to talk, because for the first time in months the periods themselves: bells, chimes, and other sonic boundaries that defined our days, were no more.

The tide of students ebbed for the last time yesterday, flowing out into the stream of buses that carried them away, and the silence is vast. Teachers talked in a relaxed, leisurely way about their summer plans: a few working summer school, some traveling, others planning further study, almost everyone working in some way to get extra income. Because of staffing cuts, far too many conversations in which I said goodbye to cool people and fine teachers I'd worked with for years, knowing with some disquiet I'd be returning to a school that had cut drama, photography, music, and wondering what that meant to the kids.

Teachers understand the slight unease we all feel in the summer: it is wonderful to rest, to know we can recharge our batteries, be with our families in both mind and body (because during the year the energy output required to be a good teacher often leaves our families with a drained hulk at the dinner table). But we also know that all this time, we may be getting a paycheck, but we're not earning money.

Before I got to The Building, I went to the coffee shop to get my last cup of the year, chatting with the kind people who kept me conscious during the school day, when that idea fully struck me. I said how nice it was to look forward to a little time to recharge, and the barista said something along the lines of "Well, we still need to come to work."

It struck me that people didn't know our summers were not a paid vacation. I told her we essentially got paid three-quarters of a salary: laid off every June, rehired each September. Hopefully. She thought for a second and said: "That's not good."

How would that realization transform the image of the teacher fishing, lying in a hammock, or taking long naps, while the taxpayer continues to foot the bill? That's right. We didn't earn any money during the summer. We got paid for 185 work days. There are 260 in a year.

As I packed up for the last time, loading up some teacher's edition textbooks, outside, through the open door at the end of the hall, I heard a lawnmower start up. The bell on my wall was silent. There was no sound of slamming lockers. 185 school days had passed, again, leaving us changed. How, I wasn't sure. Hopefully wiser and not just older, maybe better at what we did. Sometimes though, it just felt like we were done.

The kids will be waiting in September, to turn the wheel again, to learn, some despite themselves, and grow, to their astonishment. The cycle must continue.

Teachers will be there too, because it's where they belong. I'm not with them any longer, at least not bodily, but there is a part of me that will always be in and of the school, maybe the best parts of all I could become, formed in the crucible, still In The Building.

APPENDIX

Teacherese (ISD 625 dialect)

360: District Headquarters, after 360 Colborne Street in St Paul.

AP: Assistant Principal.

Early Release: The half days we used for days when we had afternoon PD.

EBD: Emotional and Behavioral Disorder. Kids who were unable to control their behavior, typically on IEPs

Formative: A quiz that doesn't count.

Grades In: The period during which you need to finalize your grades.

Hour/Period: Typically only the number is used. For example. Second, or Fifth.

IEP: Individual Education Plan. A special education document that allows a kid support for academic areas they are unable to access through the standard curriculum.

Kid: Student. Can be used s a noun. "Kid goes…"

Manipulative: Any teaching item that represents a concept-in math, dice, chips, blocks.

Master Calendar: The huge yearlong calendar on the wall in the office. Has all events in it.

MCA: Minnesota Comprehensive Assessment. The state standardized test.

Miss (Lastname): Spoken form of address for all women teachers, married or not. Staff were sometime called Miss Firstname.

Mom/Dad: Any parent.

PD: Professional development. Days teachers met as a group at school.

PLC: Professional Learning Community. A group of teachers who met to go over teaching practices in a single subject. E.g. Math, Reading, Science, etc.

Standards: Any discrete item of knowledge a student needs to acquire. "The student will be able to solve a single term algebra equation using whole numbers."

The Building: Our school.

The District: The headquarters building and the people who work in them.

Notes on dialect: Teachers typically refer to each other by their last names. The situation: an early release day, Valentine's Day, in a hallway, passing time before second period. Two teachers standing outside their doors, waiting for the bell to ring and monitoring student traffic in the halls, while watching their own rooms. A dialogue using the above language might go as follows:

Teacher 1: When's fifth today?

Teacher 2: 11:07, cause we had extended homeroom.

T1: We supposed to prep anything for PD?

T2: I don't know, the APs didn't send anything out. That's a district thing right? So is it at 360?

T1: Nope. Over at Harding. (High School)

T1; How's that MCA formative? The one the PLC made?

T2: Works ok. Took a little too long. When we have PLC I'm going to tell the coaches it needs to be shorter. Didn't really match the standard either.

T2: Where's M.? He had a sub in.

T1: He's still in the building. Someone was just covering his class. He had a meeting with Miss M. and the APs. They finally got Mom to show up for that new kid, looks like they are getting him on an EBD IEP. He moved from Iowa or something and they never did an assessment.

T1: Gotta tell you this-Gentlemen! Yes you! Walk in this hallway, please—Kid in my sixth period comes in, says-

T2: (Phone rings in his classroom) Tell me later.

T2 walks over to his doorway, answers. "This is R."

ABOUT THE AUTHOR

After stints as a journalist and in tech support, Chris Alper moved into education, working with learners of every age from Pre-K to adult. He has been an elementary school EBD aide, a middle school teacher, a district instructional coach, a teaching assistant for undergraduates and has taught at the community college level. He is currently working on the internal communications team at a software company.

Made in the USA
Lexington, KY
08 July 2018